We're All
in This Together

WE'RE ALL IN THIS TOGETHER

ISSUES AND OPTIONS IN THE EDUCATION OF CATHOLICS

Mary Perkins Ryan

HOLT, RINEHART AND WINSTON

New York   Chicago   San Francisco

Published simultaneously in Canada by Holt, Rinehart
and Winston of Canada, Limited.

LIBRARY OF CONGRESS CATALOG CARD NUMBER: 73-182769
First Edition

ISBN: 0-03-091390-X

Designer: A. Christopher Simon

PRINTED IN THE UNITED STATES OF AMERICA

TO

MONSIGNOR RUSSELL J. NEIGHBOR

with gratitude for the opportunity
to work with him on *The Living Light*
and to all its contributors
from whom I have learned so much.

Contents

Introduction   ix

1. Why Get Up in the Morning?   *1*
2. What Is "A Religious Education"?   *26*
3. Why Send Children to School?   *53*
4. What Kinds of Education Do We Want?   *69*
5. Education about Religion and Values   *88*
6. What about Catholic Schools?   *109*
7. What's Going On in "Religious Education"?   *126*
8. We're All in This Together   *147*

Introduction

IN 1964 I PUBLISHED A BOOK CALLED *Are Parochial Schools the Answer?* suggesting that to continue to pursue the ideal of "every Catholic child in a Catholic school" was not only an unrealistic course of action but also probably not calculated to build up the vital Christian communities called for by the Second Vatican Council. The furor caused by the book (probably more by its title than by what it actually said, since it was by no means a best seller) is hard to believe today. For, in the intervening years, far more basic assumptions have been questioned than that of the necessity of Catholic schools—assumptions about the "unchanging" Church, its beliefs and practices, about the worth of any existing kind of formal education, and about the validity of long-accepted Catholic and American values.

I can sympathize now much more deeply with the feelings

of those who reacted so strongly against my book than I did at the time of its publication, because I have since felt the same kind of outrage and panic at being forced so often to examine so many of my own assumptions. That the liturgy, for example —simplified and in our own language—could become by itself the chief means of Christian education for individuals and communities now seems an astonishingly naïve notion. We "litniks" worked so hard to make it a reality; things seemed so rosy when the Council's document on the liturgy was published. But now the average liturgy in the average parish seems to make even less difference in people's lives than it did before the changes. Last spring, our eighteen-year-old son came back from the Easter Vigil and said in disgust, "Mother, what's all that bit with the lights and the water got to do with me and my life?" What indeed, when the celebration took place in a kind of vacuum, at five in the afternoon, with the "participants" mainly attending to fulfill their Sunday obligation.

In writing the book about parochial schools, I frequently used the word "formation," which, I thought, had a wider meaning than "education." One of our sons wandered into my "office" one morning and looked briefly at the page I was working on. "That word 'formation,'" he said, "it sounds as though you wanted to pour people into molds, like concrete." If such molding is what any parents, teachers, and pastors have wanted to accomplish, the last few years have certainly made it clear that we have failed. Young people are not asking the questions we were trying to form them to ask, and they are not accepting the approaches to seeking answers which we tried to open to them. Should we, then, try to find more sophisticated and effective methods of "forming" the young to become good American Catholic Christians? If this were possible, would any "formation" be a realistic way of preparing young people for life in a society which, whatever else may happen to it, is changing at an increasingly rapid pace?

Such questions will not go away; on the contrary, they are

becoming increasingly urgent—what with the plight of Catholic schools and of education generally, of religious education and of churches—and people are trying to answer them from many different viewpoints and in many different ways. To many, the result seems to be complete confusion—the more so as there is now no general agreement as to what a "good American Catholic Christian" would be like. Moreover, our own "formation" seems to be constantly betraying us, even those of us who think we are most "progressive" and "radical." We find ourselves still seeking *the* answer to one or another aspect of these questions. Still worse, we find ourselves trying to impose our most recently discovered answer on persons and groups whom we influence.

But the potentially hopeful aspect of all this is that so many concerned people *are* asking questions about education and religious education, and that so many different solutions are being proposed and tried out. The present painfully confusing situation could become an increasingly creative and fruitful one if it caused us to realize that we are all called to help one another "grow up in all things toward Christ," as members of a pilgrim Church with a mission to carry out in the pilgrimage of all mankind. Growth and pilgrimage both involve the pain of leaving old securities behind, but the pain is lessened if it can be seen as part of a positive process.

Yet the realization of the possibilities of creative companionship in our journeying comes about only as we begin to share our confusions, our questions, our insights, and our solutions with one another—and also with those holding different faith-views. The tendency of most of us—especially if we are parents, teachers, or pastors—is to hide our confusions, raise our questions only with those whom we consider like-minded peers—and to impose our solutions on our children, students, or parishioners. As the last few years have shown, this tendency only leads to polarization and distrust rather than to fructifying interchange and mutual help. As we come to admit both that we are all learners and that we may have something to contribute to others' learning, we may begin to be gladdened rather than saddened by the present plurality of views and plans.

As Wayne Rood says in *The Art of Teaching Christianity*:

> Almost anywhere that two or more human beings find themselves together for any length of time in any significant way, teaching and learning are going on, for wherever there are two persons, there are differences between them, and these differences precipitate the sharing of information, know-how, wisdom and experience in a giving-and-receiving exchange.[1]

Thus the more differences, the more teaching-and-learning, the more growth of persons and groups in "information, know-how, wisdom and experience" is possible.

During the past seven years, I have been forced to admit, more than ever before, that I am a learner. Our grown and growing sons have been teaching me a great deal through their own searching and questioning. At the same time, through my work as executive editor of *The Living Light*, a Christian Education Review,[2] I have been sharing in the searching and in the information, know-how, wisdom, and experience of colleagues and contributors, of people in the field of religious education—Catholic, Protestant, and Jewish—and all the fields connected with it. Thus I have been given the opportunity to discover something of the extent and complexity of the problems involved in human and Christian education today—many of which I was happily ignorant of, or only very dimly aware of, when I wrote *Are Parochial Schools the Answer?*

This present book, then, is a mapping out of my searching and learning so far which, I hope, may serve as a conversation-starter for the sharing of confusions, questions, insights, and

1. Wayne R. Rood, *The Art of Teaching Christianity* (Nashville: Abingdon Press, 1968), p. 12.

2. *The Living Light* is edited under the auspices of the National Center of Religious Education, a department of the U.S. Catholic Conference, and published by *Our Sunday Visitor*, Noll Plaza, Huntington, Ind.

solutions among many kinds of groups: parents, teachers, administrators, pastors—separately and together; parish groups, ecumenical groups, any groups concerned with education and religious education, or in other words, with the future of mankind.

The issues which, it seems to me, need to be brought up and analyzed are deeply interrelated; we could begin with any one of them and find the others coming up sooner or later. But since a person's attitude toward life, his religious perspective, is the most fundamental question of all, it seems best to begin with a description, necessarily vastly oversimplified, of three main faith-views current among Catholics today, views which answer in three rather different ways the basic and practical question, "Why get up in the morning?" I will then go on to discuss the implications of each of these views as to what constitutes "a religious education." Chapters 3 and 4 present some of the current criticisms of our present educational system, and some of the trends and proposals for changing it, followed by a chapter on education about religion and values. Chapter 6 discusses some of the issues and problems involved in existing Catholic religious education programs, and Chapter 7 some options as to the future of Catholic schools. Finally, Chapter 8 brings together what seem to me the most hopeful lines for future development, suggesting some answers to the question, "Where do we go from here?"

Goffstown, New Hampshire

Mary Perkins Ryan

Acknowledgements

GRATEFUL ACKNOWLEDGEMENT IS made to the following publishers who have so generously granted permission to reprint from their publications:

The America Press, New York City, for excerpts from *The Documents of Vatican II*, edited by Walter M. Abbot, S.J.

The American Bible Society, for excerpts from *Good News for Modern Man*

The Center for the Study of Public Policy, for excerpts from *A Report on Financing American Education by Grants to Parents*

Harper & Row, Publishers, for excerpts from pages 23-25 of *Quo Vadimus?* by E. B. White, copyright 1930 by E. B. White, originally appearing in the *New Yorker*

The National Center of Religious Education—CCD, for excerpts of articles appearing in Volumes 1 through 6 inclusive of *The Living Light*

Our Sunday Visitor, Inc., for excerpts of articles appearing in Volumes 7 through 9 inclusive of *The Living Light*

We're All
in This Together

1
Why Get Up
in the Morning?

IN HIS WELL-KNOWN STORY *Quo Vadimus?* [1] E. B. White
stops a man on East 34th Street in the middle of New York
City and asks him, "Quo vadis. . . ? Where the hell are you
going?" The man answers:

> "I'll tell you where I'm going. I'm on my way to the Crowbar
> Building, Forty-First and Park, in Pershing Square, named
> after General Pershing, in the Grand Central zone, zone as in
> Zonite, because I forgot to tell Miss Cortwright to leave a note
> for Mr. Josefson when he comes in, telling him he should tell
> the engraver to vignette the halftone on page forty-three of
> the salesman's instruction book that Irwin, Weasey, Weasey

1. E. B. White, *Quo Vadimus?* (New York: Harper & Brothers, 1930),
pp. 23–25.

and Burton are getting out for the Frotherby-Quigley Company, which is to go to all their salesmen on the road."

"What do the salesmen sell?" I said quietly.

"They sell a new kind of shorthand course, called the Quigley Method of Intensive Speedwriting."

The author recapitulates the reason for the man's errand:

". . . because you forgot to tell Miss Cortwright to leave a note for Mr. Josefson when he comes in, telling him he should tell the engraver to vignette the halftone on page forty-three of a booklet that Irwin, Weasey, Weasey and Burton are getting out for the Frotherby-Quigley Company, instructing their salesmen how to approach people to sell the Quigley Method of Intensive Speedwriting, which in turn will enable girls like Miss Cortwright to take Mr. Josefson's dictation when he has to send a memo to the engraver telling him not to forget to vignette a halftone in a booklet telling salesmen how to sell shorthand courses. Is that correct?"

At the end of the conversation, which includes descriptions of two more equally silly ways for human beings to be spending their time and energy, that author and the man agree: why all this absurd complexity when all that anybody really wants is "a decent meal when it comes mealtime. . . . And a warm place to sleep when it comes night"?

The question "Why get up in the morning, why bother doing what I'm going to do with my day?" is one which we all face, at least occasionally. But E. B. White's story was written many years ago, before the Second World War, when Western civilization seemed to all but a few prophets to be generally on the right track, needing only a little adjusting here and there. A few thoughtful seers were trying to point out the absurdity and inhumanity of many modern types of work, but few people listened to them. The problems of world poverty, of poverty in our own country, of racism, of pollution, all very obviously existed, but it was assumed that they would be solved sooner or later by "progress." The urban crisis and the ecological crisis and international tensions were building up, but only a few cranks saw any dangers in the uncontrolled development of technology. The atom bomb had not been invented. Individuals might wonder now and then, as men have always done, about the meaning of their lives and work. But no large segments of our society were questioning, as they are now, the values and assumptions on which our culture is built.

Quite otherwise today. Older people are shocked to find that so many of the young see no use in what their parents have been doing with their lives, and begin to feel insecure themselves. Younger people ask themselves in anguish what is worth doing in this insane world which may blow itself up at any minute. Thus "Why get up in the morning? Why work at anything?" are far more real and urgent questions for more people than they have ever been before.

These questions are, of course, precisely those which religion is supposed to answer, and at a deeper level than that of "a decent meal when it comes mealtime. . . ." To many people, then, it is all the more disturbing that their religion is no longer giving them or their children clear and unambiguous answers. We used to be told that the Christian child who had learned the catechism answer to the question "Why did God make you?" was wiser than the wisest pagan sage in being sure of the purpose of his existence. But children today are being taught different answers from the one their parents learned, or no formulated answer at all—while the answer their elders learned has, for many, ceased to seem clear or helpful. What has happened to the security which gave us such an advantage over that pagan sage?

Perhaps our present insecurity indicates that we have been looking for assurance in the wrong place, in unchanging formulas and an unchanging Church rather than in the God who is with us and for us in our personal and communal history. For any formula can be understood in many different ways. I learned that "God made me to know him, love him and serve him in this world and be happy with him forever in the next" from the unrevised Baltimore Catechism, and my understanding of this answer has certainly not only developed but changed many times over the years. Yet the basic assurance which the formula was meant to convey has remained the same: God is lovingly concerned with us and has a purpose for us.

Anyone's religious development is, of course, a most personal matter. But it is a social matter too, since it cannot help being influenced by the family and the particular culture the person grew up in and has lived in. For example, a Black American way of being "a good Catholic" is not a Chicano, still less an Irish or Italian way. Observers say, for instance, that the Italian view of laws, church or otherwise, is quite different from that of American tradition; Italians look upon laws as ideals, not as rules to be obeyed literally—whether they are regulations about attending Mass on Sundays or about traffic.

Our religious development is a social matter in another way also; it is influenced by changes in our culture and by changes in the Church, itself made up of members of many different and changing cultures. All this has been true of the Church through the centuries—a fact that we unhistorical-minded Americans are likely not to take into account. If you take a look, for example, at a book reproducing pictures and statues of Christ from the earliest centuries on, in Eastern and Western Christianity, it is obvious that the people who made them thought and felt about Jesus in many different ways, and that the Christian life-styles which formed them and which they in turn helped to form were equally different.

The same is true—and why should it not be?—of attempts to develop in human thoughts and language the basic Christian assurance that God is lovingly concerned with mankind, that he shows his concern above all in Jesus, and that he conveys this assurance somehow through a historical community, the Church. These attempts have a different thrust and different emphases depending on the questions raised in different cultures and periods, and depending also on the available thought patterns and means of expression. This is true of the four Gospels themselves, which are four different presentations, from different points of view and for different immediate audiences, of Jesus' impact on those who were "with him from the beginning" of his ministry and witnesses of his death and resurrection.

Again, for example, in the second century Christians were accused of worshiping a mere man, and so Christian thinkers devoted themselves above all to explaining in terms that would be acceptable to their contemporaries that he was not only man but also God. Today we are more concerned with understanding how he was "tempted in every way as we are, but did not sin" (Heb. 4:15), perhaps to help us in our search for understanding what it means to be truly human—a concern shown both in theological writing and in such a cultural phenomenon as *Jesus Christ, Superstar*.[2]

Of course, as Scripture itself and all the great theologians agree, God's revelation of himself and his concern for mankind can never be adequately expressed in any human words or concepts or systems of thought. In the Bible, God is called Rock and Refuge, Shepherd and King, Host and Husband, Judge and Father, and many other terms signifying different human experiences and relationships. This is not only to tell us something about what he is and wishes to be to us, but also, as St. Thomas points out, to show that he is beyond all our images and ideas and symbols.

But Christians have always tended, as we do today, to forget that God is beyond all imagining and theologizing, and that consequently there can be more than one authentically Christian way of speaking about him and of trying to respond to him.

2. See the booklet, *What Do You Think of Christ?* by Edward Walsh (Dayton, Ohio: Pflaum, 1971) for a clear and readable presentation of this shift of emphasis and its consequences for Christian living today.

They tend to take the current styles of living the Christian life as the only right ones. The special vocation of many saints has, in fact, been to point forcefully to some outstanding limitations and distortions in the current style, to bring it closer to the Gospel norm, freshly perceived and interpreted in the light of the Spirit. St. Francis of Assisi, for instance, shook up the wealth-admiring Christian culture of his time with his joyous embracing of Lady Poverty. St. Thérèse de Lisieux startled the formalized and unrealistic piety of her time with the simplicity of her "Little Way."

And, of course, all through the centuries Christians trying to live their lives in cooperation with God's grace have transcended the limitations of the current thrust of Christian thinking and living. Pope John XXIII's diary shows how deeply he was imbued with the kind of pre-Second Vatican Council piety that seems so sentimental to many of us today—and yet he saw the need for opening windows to let new air into Catholic thought and life.

In the past, one dominant faith-view has shifted to another without many people being aware of it, except those actually engaged in battling for or against some aspect of the change. But in our times a faith-view different from the one in which most of us were brought up was proclaimed and urged on us in the documents of the Second Vatican Council, and still another began to emerge in the later Council documents and has been developing rapidly since the Council ended. Because of the very obvious changes in the liturgy and in regulations about fasting and abstinence, and the widespread publicity given in the media about church affairs, all Catholics who have any concern for their faith have been affected by these shifts—some less, some much more.

As a result, we are, each in his own way, engaged more or less consciously in a complex process of rejecting, resenting, examining, adapting to, accepting, and furthering these shifts. Everything has happened and is happening so rapidly that all three views coexist in the Catholic Church, in each diocese and parish and religious order—and in each of us, disturbed also, as we cannot help being, by conditions in our country and our world.

This confusion is compounded by the fact that people who are enthusiastically promoting and furthering these shifts find it all too easy to overemphasize the limitations of the "old" view. These are, naturally, the easier to recognize the longer the old view has been dominant and the greater the distance from which one can observe it; it is much more difficult to criticize a fluid, developing view objectively. Also, in the process of shifting to a new view, many values of the older view which seemed bound up with its limitations may be neglected or positively downgraded. For instance, some of the people who stopped praying the rosary years ago because it seemed part of an unreal kind of piety are now rediscovering the value of this kind of prayer in a new context.

Nonetheless, in spite of the risks and confusion involved, each generation of Christians must try to apply the Gospel test, "By their fruits you shall know them," to both inherited and developing ways of thinking about and living their faith. Here and now, asking for the light of the Spirit, we have to foster and develop those ways which seem at once most faithful to the Gospel and most suited to the needs of our times.

These shifts which we have been and are experiencing obviously have many aspects and implications. But the central significance for ordinary Catholics like ourselves, it seems to me, is precisely concerned with the question, "Why get up in the morning?" How much of our human living and experiencing is God really concerned about? How much of our daily living is included in his purpose for us? And, I think, each of the shifts we have experienced has been in the direction of enlarging our vision of his concern and purpose, so that the possibilities of full-time Christian living become greater and more realizable.

I am therefore offering the following vastly oversimplified descriptions of the answer to "Why get up in the morning?" given by each of the three current approaches. I realize that it is impossible to be truly objective. But I hope that, whether the reader agrees with me or not as to the direction of the shift, these descriptions will help him clarify his own view and compare it with those of others, to "distinguish in order to unite" [3] with those others in fruitful discussion and, perhaps, action.

The first of these views I am calling *preconciliar* rather than *traditional* because it by no means represents the rich and variegated tapestry of Christian tradition: it is simply the particular articulation of tradition that was predominant in Roman Catholicism for some time and generally inculcated by its various teaching agencies. The second can properly be called the *conciliar* view, although it was developed over many decades previously, because it is the one most clearly presented in the Council documents and in a large body of literature and teaching materials published since the Council. No better term than the *developing* view seems available for the third, since this is what it is doing, with many different emphases, through discussions, through books and articles and teaching materials and, still more, through the painful searching of many Catholic Christians.

The Preconciliar View

This view, as it seems to me now, sees God as concerned with, and present to, very little of our daily living—except when we are concerned with "holy things" or are doing what we know to be sinful. This aspect of it was brought home to me some years ago when I had a long conversation with two seniors at one of the great eastern women's colleges. Coming to such a college after an education in Catholic boarding schools had, they made it clear, been a very traumatic experience. I asked,

3. This is the subtitle of *The Degrees of Knowledge*, by Jacques Maritain.

"How?" Both said in chorus, "The absence of God." I asked, "How do you mean?" "Well," they replied, "at the convent we had daily Mass and prayers before and after class, and there were holy pictures on the walls, and visits to the Blessed Sacrament, and we were taught by Sisters . . . you know. . . . But there isn't anything of that here."

I remembered then that I had felt the same traumatic "absence" when, after three years in a Catholic boarding school, I had been sent to a physical-education school because my family thought I was too young to go to college, and again when, after three years at a Catholic college, I had gone out into "the world." And I began to wonder whether it was these painful experiences which had started me on a search for a less limited realization of God's presence and concern.

For, in the preconciliar view, reduced to its basic notions of what human existence is all about, the purpose of our lives is to save our souls—understood as meaning to save them from being punished forever in hell—and we achieve this by dying "in the state of grace." Grace is conceived as a sharing of God's own life and therefore necessary for living with him forever in heaven (in somewhat the same sense as one would need a fish's anatomy and physiology to live under water). God gave this "supernatural life," added to their human life, to our first parents. But they lost it by sin, considered as disobedience to God's command, and this loss has been passed on from generation to generation.

No human person could make up for sin, since it is an infinite offense because committed against the infinite God. So, through love for men, the very Son of God became man and, in our human nature, laid down his life in obedience to his Father, and thus made the infinite reparation needed to atone for sin and restore man to God's grace and friendship. (The theological theory underlying this view was formulated by St. Anselm, in the context of the legalistic mentality inherited with the legacy of Roman tradition, to answer the question, *Cur deus homo?*

Why did God become man? Perhaps its logical consistency, once its premises are granted, accounts for the sway it has held in the Western Church for almost a thousand years.[4]

But the grace thus regained by Christ for mankind has to be given to each person if he is to be saved. He needs also to be able to regain it if he loses it by sinning "mortally"—that is, by deliberately and consciously disobeying God in a serious way— and he should want to increase it so as to be happier in heaven. He also needs to know what God has done for him, and how to live so as to keep out of sin. Therefore, Christ founded the Church to teach men what they must believe and do in order to be saved and to make available to them the "means of grace," above all, the sacraments.

A basic limitation of this view is that it implies that getting up in the morning and doing one's day's work is positively worthwhile only for priests and Religious. After all, they are the only ones who are directly concerned with helping people realize the importance of salvation and what they should believe and do in order to be saved, and with administering the sacraments to them. Whatever part of one's day one can spend in using the "means of grace" such as attending Mass, praying the Office or the Rosary, or visiting the Blessed Sacrament, is worthwhile also. But ordinary human activities, at best, seem to be only a kind of busy-work meant to keep people occupied and out of trouble until they can die in the state of grace and get to heaven.

Thus, while American Catholics have been known the world over for their extraordinary generosity in contributing to good works under the aegis of the Church, they have at the same time and in good conscience been able to pursue the same earthly goals as the most "materialistic" and individualistic of

4. The booklet, *What Do We Really Believe?* by Rev. Richard P. McBrien (Dayton, Ohio: Pflaum, 1969) is helpful in putting this theory into context.

their neighbors. They can in good conscience spend their time and energy in as futile ways as those described in *Quo Vadimus?* while remaining uninformed and largely unconcerned about problems of race, poverty, or ecology. For "religion," as they have been brought up to understand it, has nothing to do with how one earns one's living or spends one's time, so long as one avoids sinning mortally (or repents and goes to Confession if one has done so) and uses the "means of grace" as the Church commands.

Consequently, the Church has tended to become a bulwark of any social system that allows it to teach its members what to believe and do and to provide them with the "means of grace." From this point of view, it is better if a society's legal system enforces the same moral code as the Church's, and if the dominant ethos is "religious" rather than "secular," since this makes it more "the thing to do" to obey the moral law and to believe in God. After all, once "saving souls" is seen as the overriding concern, it doesn't matter how just or unjust a social order may be, so long as it allows the Church to go about its work. True, the Church always has encouraged all kinds of institutions to relieve human suffering. But it has very seldom tried, as an organization, to change the social and economic systems that cause so much of this suffering.

This is why, as many sociologists have pointed out, religion understood in this way has tended to act, to use the Marxian phrase, as "the opium of the people." For it helps them, in view of the happy eternity to come, to endure the "breaking points" of human existence—not only pain, frustration, and death, but also injustice and all its effects. This view offers no convincing reason for trying to change conditions here on earth, since this life is only meant to be a testing place and "a vale of tears."

Of course, many Catholics today who are still convinced that this view of sin and salvation is the only authentically Christian one would reject many of its personal, social, and educational implications. On the other hand, many who accept these implications because they seem justified by this view might begin seriously to concern themselves with poverty, war, ecology, and so on, if they came to realize that another faith-view, with quite different implications, could also be an authentically Catholic Christian one, and perhaps much more so. And many others, especially young people, who are rejecting the Christian faith and the churches which proclaim it because of the implications of this preconciliar view, might see that their hunger and thirst for justice can be nourished by the Gospel when it is read in a different perspective. This is why it seems worthwhile to point out the deficiencies of this view, as we can see them now; for while its dominance in the Church is a thing of the past, it is still very much a part of many Catholics' present.

In any case, this view has never been the only one, even in the Roman Catholic Church and, for many decades before the Second Vatican Council, thinkers and doers and pray-ers were working toward the less narrow and more humanly appealing perspectives which came to predominate in the Council's documents.

The Conciliar View

In this view, the purpose of human life is to respond to the Father's love as "sons in the Son," as members of the Christian community which is Christ's Body, gathered together in the Spirit. This response is given by loving worship, which is "direct" when one prays and at its best when one takes part in the communal celebration of the liturgy, and "indirect" when one is doing one's daily work or engaging in any legitimate activity in this spirit of filial adoration, gratitude, and love.

The Good News that Christ came to proclaim was precisely that all men can, by baptism in water and the Spirit, become adopted children of God and share in his life and love, at least imperfectly here on earth and perfectly in heaven. Jesus himself is the supreme and unique exemplar of what human life lived in this way should be, both now and hereafter. His life and death were the perfect acting out, in the existing conditions of sinful mankind, of his eternal loving response as Son to the Father. In his resurrection, his human nature became perfectly "inspirited" by the Spirit and he became the "source of life to all who believe in him."

This is the life which he gives us in the Church, above all through the sacraments. Sharing his life and animated by his Spirit, Christians are to worship the Father, lovingly to serve one another and all mankind, and through their worship and service proclaim the Good News of God's love for men and the joy of sharing his life. Thus the laity in particular are to "redeem the temporal order" by taking part in everyday life in this spirit of filial love, and so reorient human life and work and material creation in and through Christ to the Father.

An almost complete change in perspective is obviously involved in making the transition from the preconciliar view to this one. (Many of the Council documents seem almost schizophrenic for this reason.) Religion is radically personalized and made communal. Sin is now seen, not so much as disobedience to laws as a refusal to respond to God's love. "Original sin" was a willed alienation from this love, a state into which we were all born but from which Christ frees us. "Grace" is not so much an ontological kind of life as a dynamic spirit: leaping fire, living water poured out in our hearts so that we may love the Father and one another "in Christ."

In this view, then, the Christian should get up in the morning to spend himself, generously and gladly, in whatever forms of direct and indirect worship his state of life calls for. When he takes part in the Mass, his daily offering of himself and his work is in a unique way united with that of the community and with Christ's perfect self-offering to the Father.

This is, surely, a beautiful view of the purpose of human existence, giving a most encouraging answer to the question, "Why get up in the morning?" It is, of course, possible to live according to this view with such a concentration on worship as to ignore the urgent realities of human life and history. For example, it is said that Pius Parsch, one of the leaders of the liturgical movement in Austria, was asked why he had done nothing to combat the rising flood of Nazism, and he answered that the mysteries of divine worship were so absorbing that he had not had time for anything else. On the other hand, and certainly in the United States, the great majority of the leaders of the various movements promoting this point of view have also been outstanding leaders in social-justice movements, seeing very clearly that the loving service of neighbor is a prerequisite to worshiping the Father "in Spirit and in truth." [5]

Nonetheless, in this view, since the highest human activity is "direct" worship and especially communal liturgical worship, a life centered in such worship and providing considerable time for it is obviously the most worthwhile. Thus some of us who enthusiastically adopted this view as married people and parents tried to adapt something like a monastic schedule of prayer to family life, and to celebrate each day in the Church's calendar in some special and appropriate way. We "cooked for Christ," [6] for instance, by confecting feast- or fast-day dishes borrowed from one or another European tradition. From this distance, such efforts seem both unrealistic (how weary to tears I used to

5. To name only a few out of many distinguished examples: Dom Virgil Michael is honored as the father of both the liturgical and the social justice movements among Catholics in this country; Msgr. Reynold Hillenbrand, one of the pioneer liturgists was also the founder of the Christian Family Movement; Rev. Thomas J. Carroll, the leader of the group in Boston known locally as "liturgical nuts," was a pioneer in the rehabilitation of blinded persons. The connection between concern for the liturgy and for social action can also work the other way around, as with the Catholic Worker movement through the years.

6. *Cooking for Christ*, the title of a book by Florence Berger (National Catholic Rural Life Conference, 1949).

get looking in flower shops in Cambridge, Massachusetts, for pine boughs to make an Advent wreath!) and superficial. But we made them in order to center, as best we knew how, our "lay" lives in the Church's liturgy.

Even though we can smile now at some of our efforts to "live the Mass," this view did encourage us to give a religious kind of attention to human life and experience. For we began to realize that Scripture and the liturgy draw on these experiences to help us understand the "mysteries" [7] of God's love. People should be urged to reflect on all the meanings of water in human life, for instance, in order to understand Baptism more fully; or of eating and drinking together in order to participate more fully in the Eucharist.

Again, this view encourages attention to human history, since it is seen as "salvation history," the history of God's loving interventions to bring men out of their state of alienation into communion with him, and with one another in him. Yet efforts on the part of the Church and its members to change social conditions and improve the quality of human life tend to be seen, in this view, not as worthwhile in themselves but as a form of "precatechesis." As St. Augustine said, one cannot preach the Gospel to people with empty stomachs. People should be fed, then, so that they will be able to hear the Gospel. Today we are in a position to see how this approach can in practice—however unintentionally—encourage a very subtle kind of rice Christianity. In any case, "redeeming the temporal order" may or may not imply trying to improve the human condition; it gives no clear imperative to do so.

In other words, this view does not seem to take human life and history really seriously. It is always looking beyond them to

7. The proper Christian meaning of the word "mystery" has, of course, nothing in common with its meaning in the term "mystery story." It means what God reveals, supremely in and through Jesus' death and resurrection. Thus sacramental celebrations were called "mysteries" as revealing God's will of love for mankind in a special way.

a God who is "up there" much more than in the midst of our daily living and suffering and struggling. No wonder, then, that it has been so difficult to communicate, except to people with a certain kind of mentality and primarily "religious" interests. To the weary man and woman with a hard and dull day's work ahead, it does not offer a very convincing reason for getting up in the morning, let alone for trying to do something to improve the quality of their own lives and those of others.

Nonetheless, this view, ultimately adopted by the Council as the dominant one, acted as a kind of lever to turn attention within the Church more directly toward the realities of human life and history. While the first document to be promulgated states: "The liturgy is thus the outstanding means by which the faithful can express in their lives and manifest to others the mystery of Christ and the real nature of the Church," [8] the last says: "Christians cannot yearn for anything more ardently than to serve the men of the modern world ever more generously and effectively . . . united with every man who loves and practices justice, Christians have shouldered a gigantic task demanding fulfillment in this world." [9]

The Developing View

Catholics who have come to see things in this perspective do so, of course, with many different emphases, and anyone who attempts to describe it cannot help presenting his or her own. But its twofold thrust seems fairly clear: God as the loving "Beyond" to be found in the midst of human experience, not apart from it; God to be served above all by serving people.

Men want fullness of life, however they may define or imagine it, and this is what God wants for them and for all creation. Why the human struggle toward greater fullness of life should

8. Constitution of the Sacred Liturgy, 2.
9. Pastoral Constitution on the Church in the Modern World, 93.

be mainly so painful and frustrated, we do not know. But we believe that, in a special way in the history of the Hebrew people and uniquely in Jesus, God—the Wholly Other whom no idea or image can grasp—reveals himself as being lovingly with and for men in this struggle. "I have come in order that they might have life, life in all its fulness" (John 10:10). In fact, it is God's presence in our personal and communal history that continually calls us out of situations that limit our development and enables us to liberate ourselves and one another for fuller, more truly human living.

What "truly human living" means concretely for persons and societies is, of course, a question with which thinkers have wrestled in every age and culture. Today it is a more crucial question than ever before, since we are becoming more and more capable of controlling people's behavior in increasingly subtle ways, and even of remodeling human nature itself. Models of anti-Utopias—of dehumanizing societies—are many, from Aldous Huxley's *Brave New World* and Orwell's *1984* to more recent stories such as Martin Caiden's *The God Machine*, in which a computer programmed to keep the human race from destroying itself went about doing so by destroying people's freedom. On the other hand, J. B. Skinner, the noted behavioral psychologist, seriously believes that we must go *Beyond Freedom and Dignity* (the title of his recent book) if we are to survive, and provided a sketch of the kind of society he envisages in his earlier *Walden II.*

Of course, it all depends on what one means by freedom and dignity, and Dr. Skinner appears to have rather superficial notions of both: equating freedom with a kind of rugged individualism which involves liberty from any restraints, and dignity with feeling superior to other people. Certainly, this is not what Christians mean by "the freedom wherewith Christ has made us free" or the dignity of the human person made to the image and likeness of God. Rather, both to the Christian and to humanistic psychologists, freedom and the dignity proper to the human person somehow involve the ability to transcend any given situation, to go beyond where one is now, to continue to grow and develop as a person, not in isolation but in community with others.[10]

Michael Novak, for instance, describes freedom as "creation out of nothingness: an act of self-affirmation, for no particular reason, out of no necessity, 'because I *want* to.'" And with it he connects three other key experiences of transcendence: *sincerity* or *honesty*, "to be honest is to create oneself anew"; *community*, "which brings into human experiences the sense of mutual creation"; and *courage*, "an often renewed evidence of our capacity to transcend what we just were, what we are." [11]

To such basic experiences of creative humanness we might add, in attempting to describe "more fully human living," those familiar (though not commonplace) experiences in which we feel most alive, our most vital and best selves. We might include experiences of intense psychophysical aliveness (more frequent in childhood and youth than in middle or old age): swimming through breakers, walking through the beauty of a spring morning. Then there are the experiences which can come at any age: of achievement, such as making something and then seeing that it is good; of discovery and delight in the beauty of nature, or of a work of art, or of a person; and, certainly, experiences of loving and being loved.

In making us feel truly human, all such experiences also in-

10. See, for example, Charles Hampden-Turner, *Radical Man, the Process of Psycho-Social Development* (Cambridge, Mass.: Schenkman Publishing Co., 1971). Chapter III, "A Model of Psycho-Social Development," begins: "Not only does man exist, but he does so in relation to others who receive his communications and witness the investment of his personality in the human environment. Hence the development of existential capacities in one man is interdependent with the development of such capacities in other men and the total relationship may be regarded as a continuous process" (p. 31).

11. "The Unawareness of God," in *The God Experience*, ed. by Joseph P. Whelan, S.J. (New York: Newman Press, 1971), pp. 8–15.

dicate a Beyond, a "more than I" to use Novak's phrase, an experience of reaching out and opening out to Ultimacy. This is the experience which religions interpret in their different ways. "We are committed to a particular religious tradition or system insofar as we are consciously convinced that it is the *expression* of the actual relationship to Ultimacy, however we think we have touched it in living." [12] To the Christian, this Ultimacy reveals itself as the loving "God and Father of our Lord, Jesus Christ."

When we have, or even recall, such experiences, we deeply feel that they indicate what life ought to be like all the time, and not only at rare moments. And so from them we can get both hints as to what "the life of the world to come" will be like and a working model of what the task of "becoming more fully human" involves. It must mean trying, in many varied ways, to develop the attitudes and abilities and conditions required in order that such experiences might form more and more of the texture of people's daily lives. It must mean struggling against the forces which limit and frustrate such development. The purpose of human life, then, is to engage in this two-fold task.

In this light, the two "great commandments" of love of God and neighbor may be seen as invitations to become more fully human. For, as was just said, experiences such as those mentioned involve a reaching out to, a welcoming of a "more than I," and Scripture confirms the insights of many modern psychologists and sociologists that a human person can develop his potentialities only through responsive interaction with others.

Such interaction, like reaching out to the "more than I," requires that we continually break out of our self-enclosedness, to be loved and served by others and to love and serve them. God's grace, then, offered to every human person, is the gift of this ability to go out of ourselves in love and, in this sense, to share

12. Robley Edward Whitson, *The Coming Convergence of World Religions* (New York: Newman Press, 1971), p. 172.

God's life, since God *is* love. Yet this God-given ability is normally mediated to us through human love. We become *responsive to* others and to God, we become responsible *for* others, by being loved and cared for by our parents, our families, other persons.[13]

In this perspective, then, "original sin," whatever its origins, consists in all the social forces and institutions, all the pressures of heredity and environment, which alienate us from one another, which make impossible, impede or distort people's ability to accept and respond to others, to develop as human persons and contribute to the development of others, to reach out and respond to the Ultimate. And personal sin is the willed refusal to love and act lovingly, willed self-enclosure, the manipulation of other persons for one's own ends, refusal or neglect to respond to others' love and to God's love, in whatever form it reaches us. "Whenever you refused to help one of these least important ones, you refused to help me" (Matt. 25:45).

Thus the work of "salvation," or liberation *from* sin and *for* the fullness of life that God desires for mankind, has been and is going on wherever people are fighting against dehumanizing and alienating pressures, conditions, situations, and institutions, wherever people are being reconciled with one another, wherever people are loving and serving one another. It is in this process that the Kingdom of God is coming.

"Community" in the sense of "mutual creation" is, then, central to becoming more human—"community" of persons and groups, to which each contributes unique riches and remains unique while sharing in the riches of the common-wealth. And the vision of such community achieved is the substance of the Christian hope in "the life of the world to come" in which God will be all in all. Of course, we can only work toward such "community"—and often with little apparent success—in our families, in the various work- and interest-groups to which we

13. Abraham J. Heschel, *The Insecurity of Freedom* (New York: Farrar, Straus & Giroux, 1959), p. 4.

belong, in our local geographical communities, our world. It is surely significant both of the lack of authentic community in our society and of our basic and intense need of it that so many attempts are being made and techniques worked out to help groups achieve "community" on one or another level—from the "community" that a working team can achieve to the total kind of "community" attempted by some communes.[14]

"Community," of course, implies some kind of sharing of interests, meaning, values, goals, services, responsibilities and resources—not necessarily all of these, but some combination of some of them. Yet unless this sharing results in "mutual creativity" of one or another kind, and a consequent reaching out beyond the bounds of the given group, then "community" can be stifling rather than fruitful. Thus here again the command to "love one another" with no bounds is ultimately normative.

God reveals the purpose of human life, God offers his grace to men in many ways and divers manners beyond any possible charting. But, we believe, he reveals himself in a special way in Scripture as desiring and enabling man's continual liberation to fuller humanness. The major enslaving and liberating experiences of human life, and those of passing from one or another kind of slavery to freedom, are precisely the main themes of Scripture, which is, as Louis Bouyer once put it, "the record of the common experience of God with mankind."

Still more, God reveals the potentialities of humanness in a unique way in Jesus. Not that we cannot learn a great deal about it from other religious leaders and traditions, from advances in human wisdom of all kinds, from history, and from the destructive and creative trends in our own times. But, through his life-style, his actions and words as given us in the Gospels, Jesus shows us the essence of true humanness in our present situation of struggle and painful development: loving

14. See the compact and interesting study, *Communes, Their Goals, Hopes, Problems*, by George R. Fitzgerald (New York: Paulist Press, 1971).

one another even to laying down our lives, loving "in deed and in truth." Nothing else that we can learn about what is truly human can contradict this basic insight, and be authentic.

And now, in his risen life, Jesus shows us something of what the full flowering of this humanness is to be. His human nature is completely charged, "inspirited" by the Spirit of God, and so "The life that he now lives is life to God" (Rom. 6:10) and equally he is available to every human person. He is present wherever people are in need, wherever people meet in his name, wherever people call upon him, as well as in the sacrament of his complete self-giving to God and to men in the signs of bread and wine.

Further, in his unique relationship with the Father, Jesus shows us how greatly God cares for human persons and how we are to respond to his love. Risen to die no more, he is the witness that God's caring for people and our attempts to care for one another will ultimately be effective. He gives us hope, since he is God's living and personal assurance that love and life will ultimately triumph over alienation and death.

In this perspective, the Church is meant to be the community of people consciously trying to work toward fuller humanness, in faith in the God and Father of our Lord Jesus Christ and his purpose for mankind, in the light and hope given in Jesus, and in the awareness of his gift of the vivifying and uniting Spirit. In their work to "serve the men of the modern world ever more generously and effectively," as the *Constitution on the Church in the World Today* puts it, Christians are "united with every man who loves and practices justice" (93). Working for human liberation and development is not a peculiarly Christian task; it is the universal human vocation. But Christians should be able to carry it out with a special freedom from limiting and simplistic visions of what humanness ought to be like, because they believe in the open future of God's promises. They should be able to carry it out with a particular patience and perseverance, because their concern for humanness draws its strength from God's own concern. And it is precisely in doing so, as individuals and as a community, that they witness to God's love for men.

Since growth toward fuller humanness requires a mutually creative community, every Christian group, small or large, as well as the Church as a whole, is meant to offer a kind of working model of such community: St. Paul's analogy of the one body which has many members is another way of saying the same thing. (The role of authority in Christian groups and the whole Church is, consequently, meant to be that implied by the origin of the term: to "increase" the creativity of the members and of the whole.)

Hence the necessity for liturgical celebrations and, most centrally, for the Eucharist. Here Christians come together to explore one or another aspect of their vocation, in the presence of Christ, in the light of God's Word. They come to say to God, "Here we are with our failures and mistakes and weaknesses. Reconcile us with you, with one another, with ourselves, with all our fellow men. Renew our freedom, enkindle our courage, share with us your own creativity, your Spirit, so that we may better be and do what you ask. In this hope, we celebrate your love." Thus liturgy, like all prayer, is not meant to provide an escape from life but, rather, a focusing of Christian faith and hope, an impetus to try to implement them less imperfectly in love.

This developing view, then, offers at once a realistic and an optimistic answer to the question, "Why get up in the morning?" It is realistic because it takes the whole of human life seriously and because it applies in any situation. It is hopeful because it opens out any situation to the Ultimate who cares for us, so that even in suffering and death we can experience freedom, honesty, courage, and community.

It is, of course, quite possible to take this view superficially, and to consider that such a shift from a legalistic morality to one based on love excuses us from the hard work of trying to love "in deed and in truth," discover what actually will best serve the well-being of all the people in a given situation, and how best to go about achieving it—the work of ethics and wise decision-making. As a friend of ours remarked drily, "We can say that God is love, but we can't say that any kind of love is God." But a considerable number of Catholics today, overreacting to their legalistic past, unfortunately tend to act as if the latter were the new Gospel. In the same way, some people who feel that their previous religious training turned them away from human experiences take the insight that God is to be found in and through experiences as meaning that they should try to make up for lost time by seeking out all kinds of experiences—turning this insight into an excuse for a kind of hedonism.

Such exaggerations or distortions then add to the fears of those who feel that the developing view is causing people to "lose all sense of the sacred," is "watering everything down to the human," or "making things too easy." Nor is the situation helped by overreactors to once-popular expressions of piety when they make people feel foolish to whom these expressions are still meaningful. One elderly lady, for instance, timidly asked her priest son, whom she had not seen for several years, "Is it still all right to say the Rosary?" What purpose had been served by causing her such uneasiness?

Those who have discovered the developing view have, then, a special responsibility, it seems to me, to continue to explore seriously both its roots in Christian tradition and its implications for behavior. Moreover, if we hope to lessen the current confusion, we all have a responsibility to explore our ideals of what a Christian, a Christian group, and a Christian church should be like, with those who seem to have different ideals from our own. And, of course, such explorations must be made in an atmosphere of respect for one another's sensitivities and convictions, and with a willingness to admit our failures to live up to our ideals, and our mistakes in trying to realize them.

I hope, then, that this presentation of what seem to me to be the three faith-views, or approaches to Christian living, current among Catholics today will contribute a little to such an exploration. We all need a great deal of patience with one another over a long period of time, especially, perhaps, in tackling the educational problems facing us. For, although it may not prove too difficult to learn to appreciate other approaches to faith as held in good conscience by others, how will we react when they try to communicate their views to our children?

2
What Is
"A Religious Education"?

MY HUSBAND'S FAMILY once had a cook from Finland who found it too difficult to master the English language (Texas version). When she was frustrated in her efforts to understand or be understood, she would stamp her foot and exclaim in exasperation, "But you no mean what I say!" This expresses fairly accurately, I think, what a great many Catholics feel today in trying to communicate with one another; we don't understand what others are saying as they mean it.

This is particularly true about matters of education. Churchgoing parents usually want their children to have the training which will equip them to live in accordance with the parents' own faith-view. Pastors would like their parishioners to live the Christian life as they, the pastors, understand it. People more or less professionally engaged in what Protestants call "Christian education" (which Catholics are now calling "religious education") can hardly help trying to communicate their own view. But what a great many people believe they want in the way of "religious education" implies many assumptions which they may not have clearly articulated themselves, although they expect other people to share them.

People who say that they want "the basics" for their children, for instance, often also want a climate of discipline, the inculcation of good habits of prayer, and regular reception of the sacraments, which in turn imply the inculcation of a whole life-style. Similarly, pastors or religious educators who want to form "Christian communities" might have in mind either a parish characterized by enthusiastic parishioners' participation in liturgical celebrations, or one known primarily for the cooperation of its members in social-action programs—the establishment of low-income, integrated housing, for instance.

The purpose of this chapter, then, is to bring out into the open the assumptions about a religious education implied by each of the faith-views just outlined, and to help the reader clarify his own views as well as to appreciate the implications of those of others.

Of course, most of us think of a religious education in terms of our own training, wanting children to gain the values that we feel we gained—the habit of praying every morning and evening, for instance—without what we now perceive to be the disvalues—for example, the fear many children felt at going to Confession. But when we were young, our parents were probably not aware of different possibilities in religious education; they mainly followed the accepted pattern, whether they liked it or not. Today, obviously, things are different, and this is why it seems important to try to understand one another's assumptions and goals, so that we will not feel so frustrated by "you no mean what I say."

In the preconciliar view, home, church, and school should combine to teach the young what they must believe and do in order to save their souls, and motivate them to do so and keep on doing so all their lives. Parents should provide a good example of obedience to the commandments and to the Church, and of using the "means of grace" regularly. The Church should provide these means, and also the preaching, teaching, advice, etc., which will enable the faithful to be sure of what the Church requires of them, and motivate them to meet these requirements. The Catholic school should provide adequate opportunities for instructing the young in their religious and moral duties. It should protect them from influences dangerous to faith and morals. It should inculcate obedience to God, to parents, and to church, school, and civil authorities. And, through its priest, Brother, or Sister teachers, visibly set apart and dedicated to God, through its schedule of daily prayer and frequenting the sacraments and overall atmosphere, it should inculcate good habits of using the means of grace and keep the children reminded of God and "holy things."

Such a religious education would, naturally, instill nonverbally the assumption that the Church, represented by the hierarchy, possesses the fullness of truth. And it would also verbally and explicitly, on higher educational levels, warn young people against the errors of other religions and philosophies, and arm them with various kinds of proofs as to the rightness of Catholic beliefs and practices and the rational bases for belief in God, revelation, Christ and the Church.

In this viewpoint, whether or not the education given in a school were generally humanizing, in the sense outlined in the previous chapter, would not be religiously important so long as it did not lead to questioning the authority and teachings of the Church. But the traditional orderly classroom model, with the children sitting quietly at their desks and the teacher imparting knowledge, is certainly more congenial to this viewpoint than an open classroom or school in which children can choose among different learning-situations and move about with a certain degree of freedom. For the school should be disciplining the children in order to keep them obedient to God and the Church, and so to make sure, as far as this is possible, that they will save their souls.

In this view, there is no need for adult religious education in any developmental sense. Adults do, indeed, need to be forcefully reminded of the truths of faith and the precepts of morality, which they should have learned as children, and motivated to live in accordance with them, through sermons on Sundays, at devotions, and through special missions. But only priests, really, need to know much more about Christian teaching than is contained in the Baltimore or some other catechism. Along the same lines, priests and bishops and the Pope, for all practical purposes, constitute "the Church." The faithful have no call to become involved in church affairs; they are simply to "pay, pray and obey."

People who hold more or less consciously to this idea of a religious education, as the kind which they themselves received and which has served them well, are unhappily finding that it is increasingly difficult to obtain for their children. The family and parish subculture—whether Irish or German, Italian or Polish—which helped give it roots and substance has largely vanished. The whole climate has changed in which it was taken for granted that parents commanded and children obeyed, pastors commanded and the laity obeyed. The changes in the Church's liturgy, regulations, and pious practices—not to speak of the birth-control controversy, news of arguments about doctrines, priests leaving their ministry, and so on—have shaken their confidence in the Church and in what it expects of them as parents and will provide for them. If "making the nine First Fridays" was so important only a few years ago, why isn't it today? Should we teach our children to say their morning and night prayers, or is that "out" too? One pastor helped draw up a restrictive convenant to make sure that the neighborhood would remain for "our kind"; now some of the Sisters don't want to teach in the (white) parochial school and are going to work in the black ghetto. How can parents with such experiences tell their children that the Church is always right when the experts whom they have always accepted don't seem to agree on what the Church teaches?

At the same time, even in areas where Catholic schools continue in relative financial security, the character of many of them generally seems to be changing. Educational innovations tend to relax discipline and lead to the questioning of authority. Priest and Religious teachers are disappearing, and when they are still found in schools they tend to dress and act more and more like lay people.

Still more disturbing, in a number of school and out-of-school religion programs, the teachers and materials used seem to encourage young people to downgrade their elders' values, opinions, and religious practices, rather than supporting parents and parental authority. Almost nowhere do these programs seem to be teaching the basic truths of Christian faith and precepts of morality.

It does not solve such people's problems to be told that they do not understand modern pedagogical methods, that there has been a great deal of research to prove that young children cannot grasp abstract formulations, and that making them memorize such formulations may positively harm their future religious development. Bewildered parents certainly should be introduced to the pedagogical and psychological rationale behind new educational methods. But they should also be introduced to the Christian perspective which is the rationale for adopting these methods in religious education.

If the school or program is no longer trying to produce the preconciliar kind of Catholic which the parents expect it to, they should have its aims clearly presented to them and be given adequate opportunities to discover that these are also authentically Catholic Christian ones. This does not mean, of course, that those conducting the school or the program should compromise their own viewpoint; it means, rather, that they should neither conceal it among generalities about "modern methods" nor try to impose it, but explain it and try to bear witness by living in accordance with it. Any other course seems unfair, unwise, and unchristian.

Those pastors and parents who, like my husband and myself, enthusiastically adopted what was described in the previous chapter as the conciliar view, when it was being shaped in the decades before the Council, thought of "a good religious education" as a process to be carried on primarily in the parish church and the home, with the help of the school. Home reading and study of Scripture, family prayer along the lines of a much simplified monastic "Hour," family celebrations of the Church's feasts and seasons would complement and extend into family living the parish's liturgical celebrations, and both together would provide the basic religious education "curriculum" for adults and children alike. Through such an education, they would grow in the realization that their whole lives were meant to be "religious," reminding them in one way or another of the Mystery of Christ, and providing the material for the "spiritual sacrifice" to be offered in loving praise with Christ's offering at Mass.

Some of us, as I mentioned in the previous chapter, went to what now seem like absurd lengths in trying to practice home "liturgical piety."[1] One heroic couple I know managed to impose a monastic "great silence" on their large family after evening prayers. Some even tried to have communal family prayer seven times a day. Nonetheless, the idea that adults and children together should be involved in an ongoing educational effort as members of the Christian community was a sound one, and an idea which is now at least beginning to be more widely considered and implemented.[2]

1. The title of a pioneering work by Louis Bouyer, published by the Notre Dame University Press in the early 1950s.
2. A most interesting example is the "family clusters" initiated by Margaret Swain, "teaching minister" of First Baptist Church in Rochester, N.Y. Four or five families gather weekly for open-ended learning experiences, facilitated by a trained leader. Three such clusters meet at First Baptist, and the idea is spreading in Rochester and elsewhere. See Edna Stumpf, "Clustering in Rochester," *Colloquy*, vol. 4, no. 11 (December, 1971), pp. 31–33.

Educators who shared the same vision thought of the Catholic school, or catechetical program for children, as furthering the formation of the young through the same kinds of prayer and celebration, and through more formal instruction in what began to be called "kerygmatic" (from the Greek word *keryx*, meaning herald) catechesis. In other words, the teacher should "herald" the good news, training children, according to their capacity, to appreciate Scripture, to take part wholeheartedly and intelligently in the liturgy, to understand the major doctrines of the faith in the Good News perspective, and to witness to God's love in their daily lives, after the example of the saints.[3]

But it has seldom happened, before or after the Council, that the families, the school and/or the Confraternity of Christian Doctrine (CCD) program, and the priests and Religious of a parish all shared and tried to implement the conciliar view of a religious education. (We ourselves moved three times in ten years in search of such a parish and school and group of like-minded parents.) Thus, in all but a few favored places, the strength which a united effort might have generated has largely been lacking. The conciliar view has never really been given a fair try through the cooperation of all the Catholic agencies concerned.

This lack of response to the Council's directive has often been blamed on a lack of leadership on the part of bishops, apathy on the part of priests, and so on. But it is a real question whether, with all the zeal and resources and tact imaginable, this view could have ever been widely incarnated in modern American life. For it presupposes not only the cooperation of

---

3. Scripture, liturgy, doctrine and witness were seen as the four "signs" through which God reveals himself and his plan for mankind. In the Decree on the Pastoral Office of Bishops in the Church of the Second Vatican Council, "scripture, liturgy, tradition and the magisterium, and the life of the Church" are named as the "bases" or "sources" of catechetical instruction (14).

families, pastors, and schools, but also a culture favoring, rather than distracting from, regular times for family prayer, the observance of the Church's feasts and seasons, a peaceful concentration on "the things of God"—a culture which would quite obviously be very different from our own. To take a simple example on the external level, we all know when it is Christmastime and, to a lesser extent, Easter, because commercial interests see to it that we can't ignore these Christian feasts. But our culture doesn't help us live in the spirit of Advent or Lent or the Easter season.

If the key word in the preconciliar view of a religious education is "inculcation" or "indoctrination," the key word in the conciliar view is "formation" to a living and flexible, but fairly well-defined model of an active member of "the people of God." And to "form" requires at least a considerable amount of control over all the major influences in people's lives, as novices used to be formed in convents and seminarians in seminaries. But even if we were all agreed it was desirable, parents, schools, and parishes all together could not exercise such control over young people's lives today.

On the other hand, to the extent to which this view has influenced Catholics' thinking, it has opened up possibilities of a sympathetic study of other Christian churches, their liturgies, and their approaches to Christian education and to "an acceptance of their members with respect and affection as brothers." [4] Through its emphasis on the Bible, it also opened up new possibilities of religious dialogue with Jews, difficult and painful as such dialogue may often be, due in part to the very different perspectives in which Christians and Jews view the sacred books and the too common Christian insensitivity to this vast difference. But at least more real respect began to be extended to all religions, and an eagerness to find what is "true and holy" in them, to "acknowledge, preserve and promote the spiritual and moral goods" possessed by their followers "as well as the values

4. Decree on Ecumenism, 3.

in their society and culture." [5] Once the defensiveness of the Roman Catholic preconciliar view began to break down, the way was opened to the idea that a religious education could and should include opportunities to become acquainted with the beliefs and practices of other religions—and with the people who hold them.

Again, the aims of "kerygmatic" catechesis made it necessary for catechists to reconsider the "how" of religious education. True, the emphasis was still very strongly on "content," in the sense of an amount of information to be absorbed. But to appreciate Scripture, to take part intelligently in the liturgy, to witness to God's love in daily life are all *abilities*—and abilities cannot be cultivated simply by the memorization of facts and formulas. So questions began to be asked about how best to cultivate these abilities in people of different ages, and different methods were enthusiastically tried out.

In the same way, the importance of the teacher's style and attitude became increasingly evident. A filial love of the Father cannot be communicated by someone who is himself unloving; a sense of belonging to the community of the Church cannot be communicated by someone who distrusts human relationships.

Equally, the role of human experience in religious education began to be seriously considered. A person who has never had to seek refuge from serious danger can hardly appreciate the psalms which speak of "God, my Rock and my Refuge"—even though he might appreciate them without any personal acquaintance with the rocky terrain of Palestine and kind of guerrilla warfare it facilitates. On a much deeper level, someone who has never had the experience of being forgiven and reconciled lacks the basis for appreciating the sacrament of Penance; a person who has had no strong and loving father-figure in his life lacks the prerequisite for relating to God as Father. In this view, the emphasis is on human experiences as valuable for

5. Declaration on the Relationship of the Church to Non-Christian Religions, 2.

helping us appreciate Scripture and the sacraments and what they reveal of God and his loving dealings with us in Christ. The cycle was not completed, though it was suggested in the idea of "living the Mass": that Scripture and liturgical celebrations should in turn illuminate, judge, rectify, and enlarge our human experiences. All the same, the way was opened for this further development.

Perhaps the most important effect of the conciliar view and its promulgation by the Council was to turn the attention of an increasing number of Catholics to the need for adult religious education. For a long time before the Council, prophetic voices like that of Frank J. Sheed had been calling for a growing, maturing kind of "faith seeking understanding," and insisting that ordinarily intelligent people, with or without college degrees, were capable of such growth, whether they were priests or not. I remember Mr. Sheed's vast amusement many years ago when I pointed out to him the conclusion of an article in *Theological Studies* by Fr. Murray, arguing for different kinds of courses for college students and adults from those given in seminaries, and using the analogy (I quote from memory): "You wouldn't expect the sheep to be invited to sit at the same table with the shepherd or ask the shepherd to get down and crop the grass with the sheep." In spite of the mentality represented by this analogy, the idea of the desirability of adults continuing to mature as Christians, intellectually and otherwise, did spread through various movements of the past thirty years—the Christian Family Movement, for example—even though it hardly touched the majority of the clergy and laity.

Today, the changes inaugurated by the Council and the many forms of unrest in the Church have made it obvious that Christian adults, clergy and laity alike, can no longer be ignored in any responsible consideration of the scope of the Church's educational mission. Adult religious education is now given at least lip service at every level, though many different things may be meant by the term. The shepherd/sheep mentality is still all too dominant, not so much dividing the clergy from the laity, but dividing the teachers from the to-be-taught: "How can *we* get at *them?*" But, as we shall see in the remaining chapters in this book, many trends are combining to develop the idea of a Christian community, old and young together, helping one another in various capacities to "grow up in all things toward Christ" and to implement this idea in practice.

Thus the conciliar idea of a religious education opened the way to several vital developments. But, just as it was becoming respectable after the Council and had begun to be incarnated in official changes in the liturgy and in texts and teaching materials, the basic unrealism of the theological viewpoint on which it was based began to dawn on even some of its most enthusiastic promoters, for many different reasons. Pastors found their parishioners less than enthusiastic about "taking active part" in the liturgy. Catechists discovered that young people could be just as bored by "salvation history" as by catechism formulas. Far more significantly, the flaw in its "God-up-there" emphasis on worship became increasingly evident.

For example, when I went to the Liturgical Week in Houston in August, 1966, I met a friend from New Zealand who, when driving across Texas, had been horrified at encountering several pathetic groups of migrant workers marching to the state capital through the dust and heat to protest their grievances. "If you people were really serious," he said indignantly, "you'd call this whole Week off and get out of your air-conditioned rooms and go join those workers. Didn't the Lord say that he doesn't want our worship until we have been reconciled with our brothers? And there's quite a bit in the Bible about God's wanting justice more than sacrifices, and about people who say, 'Lord, Lord,' and don't do his will. . . ."

The incongruity, which my friend stated so forcefully, between the plain teaching of Scripture and the kind of "religiousness" that we had been cultivating has come home more and more strongly to many of us in the events of the past few years. A growing realization of Christians' individual and communal responsibility for the increasingly obvious ills of our society has made us look for and welcome the contributions of theologians and philosophers, of sociologists and psychologists, of teachers and doers of the Word to what I have been calling the developing view of Christianity and to the religious education which it implies.

This education, it now seems evident, needs to be one which neither encourages Christians to be unthinkingly immersed in, and at the mercy of, their society and culture, except for certain sacred actions and moments, *nor* is set apart from it by an artificially created "Christian culture." It needs to be an education which encourages and aids Christians to take a critical and constructive part in their society and culture. The goal is to make more fully human living, as sketched in the previous chapter, more possible for more people.

A religious education, in such a framework, would include providing people with adequate opportunities, suited to their age and particular needs and talents, to cultivate the abilities required for truly human and humanizing living and acting. In the two following chapters we will, therefore, discuss some of the major criticisms being leveled against our present educational system as precisely discouraging the development of many of these qualities—such as the ability to wonder, to delight, to play, to create, to make wise decisions, to act freely and responsibly, to form authentic communities in Novak's sense of "mutual creation" mentioned in the previous chapter—and some of the experiments and proposals to improve education in our society.

Such an education would also provide people with opportunities to locate their own tradition in the context of the whole human search for meaning and wholeness, and to become acquainted with the manifestations of this search in the cultures, ethical systems, and religions of mankind. Thus Christians would come to see themselves, not as exempted from this search, but as contributors to it from within: members of the pilgrim human race in being members of the pilgrim Church.

Obviously, the elements of a religious education so far mentioned are equally elements of a truly human education. (In Chapter 5, we discuss the desirability and feasibility of including education about religion and values in everyone's education, whether in private or public schools.) Thus, in this view, Christians and non-Christians can and should work together toward types of education that would enable each person to develop his unique potentialities as a person and as a member of various communities. This is the kind of education called for by Roger Garaudy, the French Marxist:

> As far as faith is concerned, whether faith in God or faith in our task, and whatever our difference regarding its source— for some, assent to a call from God; for others, purely human creation—faith imposes on us the duty of seeing to it that every man becomes a man, a flaming hearth of initiative, a poet in the deepest sense of the word; one who has experienced, day by day, the creative surpassing of himself—what Christians call his transcendence and we call his authentic humanity.
>
> This ideal is exalted enough and difficult enough of achievement to demand the combined efforts of all of us, even if we have to see the burning away—in the fire of dialogue which allows us to meet, deep within ourselves, on the threshold of the basic—of everything which prevents us from becoming what we are.[6]

Thus in working in whatever ways are open to us—as citizens, as parents, as teachers, as organizers, through different kinds of groups and organizations—to make more opportunities for a more humanizing education available to everyone, we are at

6. Roger Garaudy, *From Anathema to Dialogue* (New York: Herder and Herder, 1966), pp. 123–124.

once helping to provide our fellow Christians with essential elements of their total religious education and carrying out our vocation of service to society in a most vital area.

Equally, in this view, non-Christians can contribute to the religious education of Christians. What is required is not Christian, or specifically Catholic, agencies but, rather, persons or agencies who share the same general ideas of humanness and are working effectively to achieve them. A teacher who, in a climate of respect for the children and wonder at what mathematics can reveal of reality, helps Catholic young people develop their mathematical abilities is contributing to their religious education, whether he knows it or not and whether he is a believer or not. A community organizer who helps a group of welfare mothers learn how to work together to improve their particular situation is contributing to their religious education, whatever his personal beliefs.

Then what, in this perspective, are the specifically Christian aspects of a religious education? They cannot be a kind of frosting on a humanistic cake, to be added to something already complete in itself. They must, rather, provide the permeating flavor which gives the cake its unique taste. The following lengthy quotation is taken from a document concerned specifically with programs that used to be called "catechetical" and are now more commonly referred to as "religious education." [7] But I think that it has a wider reference to the kind of educating that can be carried out, not only through such programs,

7. This document, published in *The Living Light,* vol. 6, no. 2 (Summer, 1969) under the title "The Sources of Catechesis and Their Use," was prepared under the auspices of the National Center of Religious Education as the contribution of the Church in the United States to the work of the Commission set up by Pope Paul to work out international catechetical guidelines. These guidelines were published by the Sacred Congregation for the Clergy in 1971, and are available under the title of *General Catechetical Directory* from the Publications Office of the U.S. Catholic Conference, 1312 Massachusetts Ave., N.W., Washington, D.C. 20005.

but also in homes and parishes and groups in many ways, and that has the greatest potential for helping Christians of every age consciously and intentionally to "grow up in all things towards Christ." (The "sources" of catechetics referred to are those named in the Second Vatican Council document on the Pastoral Office of Bishops: Scripture, liturgy, tradition and the magisterium, and the life of the Church.)

THE FUNCTION OF THESE SOURCES IN THE CATECHETICAL TASK

From what has been said so far, it should be clear that the function of these "sources" in catechesis is determined by their function in the life of the individual Christian and of the Christian community. The catechist is not only to teach Christians about these sources, but especially to enable Christians to bring the light of these sources to bear on their own experiences and those of their fellowmen.

Thus, the catechist will try to help his students hear the scriptural Word of God in such a way as to shed light on one or another aspect of their own experiences, and the present situation of the Church and mankind, so that they may put that word into living practice. He will try to show them "faith seeking understanding" in the development of doctrine through the ages in such a way as to encourage their own faith to seek greater understanding, as members of the community of the Church which is growing towards "the perfect knowledge of Jesus Christ." He will try to help them participate intelligently and actively in Christian worship "in spirit and in truth." He will try to show them how the life of the Church and its members in past ages and cultures, with its achievements, its mistakes, and its failures, sheds light on the problems and the mission of the Church today. He will try to put them in living contact with persons who are witnessing to God's love by their service of human needs in one or another area of human life, and to help them enter into communities which are trying to give such witness. He will try to open out to them the requirements, dimensions, and possibilities of this witness in their actual situations. In short, he will try to help them to "know Christ" in every area and aspect of their lives.

THE USE OF THESE SOURCES

1. "LIFE-THEMES"

The whole experience of being human is to be transformed in Christ, delivered from the ambiguities and limitations of unregenerated human nature—that is, from the power of death in the widest sense—into the "glorious freedom of God's sons," into the freedom, above all, to love as Christ loves. The work of catechesis must, therefore, basically consist in many-sided explorations of this experience of being human in the light of the sources discussed above.

Obviously, how this can be done with any given group will vary in accordance with their abilities and situations. . . . But, generally speaking, the method which seems most in harmony, at once with the nature of Christianity and with the insights of modern psychology and pedagogy, is to organize catechetical programs around an exploration of major human experiences or "life-themes," which are equally the main themes of scripture and liturgy, explicated in various ways by Christian tradition.

These themes are to be explored in the context of the uniquely biblical theme of dynamic history made possible by God's identification with human history from the very beginning, and uniquely manifested in the Incarnation. Because, in the risen Christ, God is with and for men in their struggle for personal and social fulfillment, all personal and social history is to be seen as oriented toward the transcendent fulfillment of human hopes in the eschatological Kingdom of God. This eschatological theme also implies the complementary theme of personal dialogue between God and men, a dialogue in which God graciously takes the initiative.

These themes might be listed, described, and developed into a complexus of ancillary themes in many different ways, since they are interdependent and since each has, in the concrete, so many psychophysical and social components. Merely to give an idea of the possibilities of this approach, we might list the following major themes, with some of their biblical counterparts:

POSITIVE HUMAN EXPERIENCES AND THEIR NEGATIVE COUNTERPARTS

Life: growth, development, sense of self-identity and self-worth, vitality, fulfillment, light, "spirit" in the biblical sense.

Death: stultification, illness, crippling, inadequacy, weakness, frustration, darkness, "flesh" in the biblical sense.

Love: self-identity and self-worth, human development achieved only by being loved and loving, sense of presence, reverence, recognition of worth of other; justice, law, development of personal conscience and conscience of mankind, self-giving and service. God's loving-kindness, the two great commandments, love the fulfilling of the law.

Egoism: imprisonment in self, exploitation of others (and of material things), counterfeits of love; sin and sins, idolatry, disobedience, hard-heartedness, refusal to love and be loved, injustice.

Community: true order, peace in the biblical sense of fullness of human well-being in community, in right relationship of love of God and one another, social justice, covenant, People of God, Church, Kingdom.

Alienation: injustice, divisiveness, prejudice, consciousness of guilt, refusal to forgive, "the world" in the pejorative sense.

Freedom: mature ethical conduct as free response to God's love, effectiveness in serving others, responsibility, freedom from limitations to love as Christ loves.

Slavery: to sin, to obsessions and compulsions, to prejudices, to legalism, to conformism, to "principalities and powers," to sin.

Creativity: use of human powers and material things for glory of God and good of others, need for discipline and encouragement.

Repression: disappointment, frustration, failure, misuse, waste.

Delight: in nature, human works, other persons, God; gratitude, praise, sense of creatureliness as relationship to transcendent "Thou."

Disgust: sorrow, sense of contingency as existential anguish, pain.

Hope: personal, social, cosmic; God's fidelity to his promises.

Despair: sense of meaninglessness—personal and historical.

EXPERIENCES OF TRANSITION: CONVERSION, FAITH, SALVATION, REDEMPTION, EXODUS, PASCHAL MYSTERY

from darkness to light,
from sickness to health,
from danger to security,
from alienation and loneliness to love and community,
from hatred to forgiveness, reconciliation,
from war and divisiveness to peace,
from anguish to joy,
from death to life.

EXPERIENCES OF MINISTRY

Election, vocation	Making
Forgiving	Exercising authority
Discerning (prophet)	Preaching
Deciding	Teaching
Serving	Witnessing
Mediating	

It should be noted that in exploring such life-themes, or any of the subsidiary themes which might explicate and enrich them, the catechetical effort should not terminate with the student's increased understanding of, for example, the paschal mystery, through an exploration of deliverance in his own experience and the experiences of others (through films, pictures, stories, etc.). It should go on to help the students see their own lives, the situations they live in, and the situations of their society and the world, in the light of the paschal mystery. This illumination should then give new urgency and new hope to the works of deliverance which the students might undertake or encourage (for example, to deliver themselves and others from some crippling form of prejudice), and a new empathy with the persons and forces working for one or another kind of deliverance for one or another group, or class, or nation. In the same way, the worship-experiences of the students should, generally speaking, follow the basic pattern of the Eucharistic Prayer, praising and thanking God for his wonderful works in behalf of mankind and asking him to complete his work in the coming of the Kingdom.

Thus, these explorations should not only be ordered to a better understanding of human life in the light of Christ. They should also, directly or indirectly, aid students to evaluate human behavior in the light of the norms of human and Christian wisdom and to develop toward moral maturity. Equally, these explorations should open out the possibility of meeting with God in all places and at all times and of responding to him with spontaneous movements of mind and heart, as well as with formulated prayers, both personal and communal. Sensitively carried out, this approach to catechesis should foster the spirit of reverence, awe, wonder and contemplation, as well as of the active and effective love of neighbor which is the fulfilling of the law. . . .

I hope that this quotation goes to show, among other things, the perennial relevance of Scripture, properly used as illuminating our own experiences and not reduced to "Bible stories" or "Bible history." The fact that its images and background are not those of urban twentieth-century culture need not detract from this relevance if the image is related to the deep human experience which it represents and then to the manifestations of this experience in people's lives today.

For example, a course in the prophets might not seem a very helpful exercise for high school or college students. But an imaginative teacher worked out a unit in which the class began by considering the work of contemporaries whom many consider as prophets: persons who have forcefully been calling our attention to the ills of society as they see them and saying what ought to be done about them if we are to escape disaster. The class examined the words and works of Martin Luther King, William Buckley, Daniel Berrigan, Billy Graham, Malcolm X, and Caesar Chavez; then it turned to the Hebrew prophets in the context of the analogous problems their society was facing. Ultimately, what the students learned from the "speaking for God" (which is what "prophecy" really means) of the biblical prophets became their criterion for distinguishing between true and false prophets today. Similarly, an imaginative Jewish educator organized a campaign with a high school group running the prophets for President, which meant that the students had to find out what each candidate stood for and apply it to present-day issues.[8]

Once I was on the lecture platform with the distinguished co-author of a series of religion texts when someone in the audience sharply questioned the meaningful use of biblical images, whether in the liturgy or elsewhere, when dealing with modern young people. The author agreed entirely, insisting that these images are mainly meaningless, and went on at some length on the special irrelevance of talking about sheep and lambs to urban children who saw such creatures only occasionally on a trip to the zoo. I returned from my lecture and was cooking supper when our sixteen-year-old son (six feet three and broad in proportion) burst in from school to tell me at some length how "neat" and "cool" he found the Good Shepherd psalm, which they had been reading in his nonsectarian school. "But,

8. See Daniel Brown, "Teaching the Old Testament to American Students," *The Living Light*, vol. 5, no. 4 (Winter, 1968–69), p. 65, and Audrey Friedman, "On the Campaign Trail with the Prophets," *The Living Light*, vol. 9 no. 1 (Spring, 1972), in press.

dear," I said feebly, "you don't know anything about sheep. . . ." "What difference does that make?" he answered, and went about his business. So I do not think that we need discard Scripture because it doesn't mention airplanes and mesons. We need, rather, to cultivate children's imaginations, and their ability to respond to the implications of poetic writing and speaking.

This is why, it seems to me, the results of Ronald Goldman's research published in his *Religious Thinking from Childhood to Adolescence* (Seabury Press, New York City), which have had a wide influence on religious educators, need to be taken with considerable reservations as applied to their "readiness" for many parts of the Bible. He tested children's verbalized understanding of several Bible stories at different ages, and found that it corresponded to the stages of cognitive development worked out by Jean Piaget, which are more or less generally accepted. Normal children are capable of "concrete operational thinking" from 7 to 11 years, but only begin to develop "formal operational thinking"—the ability to handle abstract concepts such as "being" or "substance"—from pre-adolescence on.

But the abilities to wonder, to feel awe, to respond to beauty, to sense mystery, are not "cognitive" abilities in Piaget's sense and cannot be measured by such tests. Whatever we should call them, they are vital to truly human development, and are nourished by poetically told stories and legends and by all the arts, as well as in more indirect ways. Of course, it is all too possible to present Bible stories in wrongly simplified, prosaic language and under conditions discouraging any sense of wonder, and I would agree with Dr. Goldman that to do so is as unhelpful to children as giving them abstract doctrinal formulas. But they don't have to be presented this way. I remember vividly my awe and delight in the tremendous imagery of the Apocalypse, read aloud by my mother on summer evenings when I was nine or so—thank God, nobody dreamed of asking me what it "meant" any more than what the poems "meant" that I read or had read to me at the same age. And I am sure that many people who were thus properly introduced to Scripture (and other kinds of great literature) as children have had the same experience. For all these reasons, then, I do not believe that the Bible need be "out" for modern children or adults. It has been "in" for a very long time, in many cultures, precisely because it is such a *human* word of the *mystery* of God's relationships with mankind.

In using this approach in structured religious education programs, it must, of course, be adapted to the person's age and capabilities. As the document just quoted goes on to say:

> . . . the catechetical effort with young children, whether carried out by their parents or a catechist, should consist in providing them with multiple and, occasionally, structured and intensified concrete experiences of the basic elements of nature and healthy human nature in such a way that the loving and creative presence of God is opened out to their immediate intuition.

Thus parents' primary contribution to their children's religious education is to try to bring them up as maturing human persons who are aware of, open to, awed and fascinated by God's loving self-communication as they come to know him and about him in various ways. This contribution is one in which the parents' own attitudes toward God, one another, and all the realities of human existence inevitably play the major part, since these attitudes are what most deeply shape the children's. Parents, then, can use this same "catechetical" approach with their children—and many do without identifying it as such—by their own attitude of loving attention to their children and of wondering attention to God's presence in different situations, as well as by such verbalizings as "Isn't God good to give us such a beautiful sunset!"

As to the value of various forms and amounts of family

prayer, home celebrations, and other explicitly religious activities, the best criterion seems to be what seems authentic and helpful to the particular family. Suggestions offered by pastors and religious educators may open out new possibilities along these lines. The thought-and-action-provoking book, *Children's Liturgies,* for instance, published by The Liturgical Conference, offers a wide range of suggestions for home as well as for other uses. But the "one thing necessary," surely, is that the parents are *trying* to love one another, their children, their fellowmen, and God, that they are *trying* to develop as Christian persons themselves and to help their children do so in whatever ways seem most suited to their capabilities and circumstances. The one thing which all our grown children agree was good about their upbringing, for instance, was their father's reading them stories and poems, including ones from the Bible. Our attempts at family prayers and celebrations never seemed to come off, somehow—and we envied the families for whom they did. But at least this family reading was a real influence in *our* children's lives.

Family religious education, however a given family may carry it out, might then be complemented by a structure program (perhaps every week, perhaps more rarely) and, ideally, happy experiences of worship, to help children come to adolescence familiar with their Christian heritage, with prayer, and with the main thrust of Christian living. (See chapter 7 for a further discussion of children's "religious education.")

Programs for adolescents might not only continue to use this same approach, but also supplement it with courses in, say, the development of the central Christian doctrines through the ages, and in ethics as applied to daily decisions. Whatever is offered should assist them to rethink their childish faith and to understand the meaning of a personal free commitment to lead the Christian life as a member of the community of the Church.

This kind of religious education does not aim to inculcate Christian beliefs and practices or to "form" children to any predetermined model of what a Christian should be. People cannot be forced or even formed to be "committed" Christians. Obstacles to commitment can be removed, aid given, and resources provided. The Christian vision of the meaning and potentialities of human personal and communal liberation and development can be opened out and explored. Above all, to "grow up in every way toward Christ" can be made to seem worthwhile by the life-styles of people who are trying to do so. But to follow the Christian "Way" must ultimately be each person's free choice, made and remade throughout life, in conscious preference to other life-styles and interpretations of life's meaning.

This same kind of approach can obviously be used by individuals; in fact, the aim of providing this kind of religious education during childhood and adolescence should be precisely to equip the person to continue his own religious education along the same lines all his life, with the help of fellow Christians.

It can also be used in various ways by adolescent and adult groups to bring their common experiences and actions and the social structures in which they are involved into the light of God's Word and God's presence, and motivating them to further growth and effort to improve these structures. For example, let us consider a group concerned with helping paroled prisoners. They began to hold regular meetings in which the problems involved were explored with expert help, and concrete plans were made for action. The group ended each meeting with a period of reflection on the Gospel value involved in this specific situation, leading to an increased understanding of the Christian stance toward social evils, and prayer that they would be able to act more effectively in the Spirit, with God's love for all men. The progress of this group has been presented as an example of what one writer calls the "action-reflection" method:

Explicit theological reflection has an essential role in the action-reflection method, since in social action situations the religious dimension many times controls the action. Two common examples are the religious validation of a fear of conflict and of the belief that a person's poverty is due to his own fault and the will of God. The use of power will always cause conflict and polarization. Someone who has been educated to fear conflict and polarization, as opposed to the gospel message of love, will shy way from their use. His fear is real and is based on his religious education. The theological resource person present in the group must be able to deal with this religious value. The same is true of seeing poverty as God's will; the Calvinistic work ethic and the image of God as the one who inflicts us with pain and poverty as a punishment for our sins must be exposed as false.[9]

Along similar lines, the noted religious educator Pierre Babin defines catechesis as "the act by which a group gains awareness, in the light of the Gospel, of the process of the total development of mankind in which it is called to take part."[10] He suggests further that "catechesis" for adolescents and adults should mainly consist in helping groups come to a realization of their real needs and limitations of one kind or another, and of what they can do about them here and now; only in this context should the Christian faith in the God who wants men to have life in abundance be opened out to them. In other words, groups should be concretely engaged in some aspect of the work of human liberation and development if they are to appreciate, and make their own, God's concern for it.

This approach can also be used by communities with members of all ages, as several experimental or "floating" parishes have been doing.[11] Since it is in effect a development of the

9. Nathan Kollar, "Doing Christianity: The Action-Reflection Method," *The Living Light*, vol. 8, no. 1 (Spring, 1971), p. 87.

10. Pierre Babin, "Towards a Catechesis of Human Development," *The Living Light*, vol. 8, no. 1 (Spring, 1971), p. 72.

11. See, for example, Fred and Linda Beauvais, "Catechetics in Community: A Program with Growing Pains," *The Living Light*, vol. 5, no. 3 (Fall, 1968), p. 30; Connie Comstock, "An Experimental Program for the Children of an Experimental Parish," *The Living Light*, vol. 4, no. 4 (Winter, 1967), p. 19; Joseph Dillon, "An Experiment in Parish Religious Education," *The Living Light*, vol. 7, no. 3 (Fall, 1970), p. 132.

Service of the Word, these communities use it as such, as introductory to the Eucharist. The adults, adolescents, and children in different age groups meet separately and consider the same theme taken from the liturgy of the Sunday or season, each group in its own fashion, and then all meet together for the Eucharist.

Thus, during the Easter season, for example, the theme of the hope of new life given us by Christ's resurrection might involve the adults in a discussion of practical ways of improving local discriminatory real-estate practices. The adolescents might be encouraged to explore, perhaps through role-playing or a film, the real and pseudo experiences of new life that come with "falling in love." And the younger children might be provided with actual experiences of new life, through photographs or slides of growing creatures or, still better, by going out into the springtime and taking in its "newness" through all their senses, and then drawing or painting or dancing what they had experienced.

This approach can also be used in parishes, dioceses, and whole areas as an extension of and preparation for the Sunday Mass, as is done in the "Co-ordinated Catechetical Program" developed by the East Asian Pastoral Institute.[12] A theme taken from the liturgy and relevant to the people's immediate concerns is developed through all the available media in various ways and is the theme of all religious instruction programs throughout the week, of adult groups, etc., and of the Sunday sermons. The final chapter of this book will outline some further possibilities of this community approach to Christian education which seem to offer hope for ordinary parishes as well as special groups.

In another chapter, we shall also discuss some of the major problems that have been caused by, or encountered in, attempts to implement this developing view in school and out-of-school programs. The most obvious obstacle, is that although this view

12. See Jose M. Calle, *Catechesis for the Seventies* (Manila: East Asian Pastoral Institute, 1970).

of a religious education encompasses so much more than just programs in schools and for the young, most people still assume that these must be the chief means of education of any kind and that education *is* mainly for the young. In this, the developing approach is in harmony with a conviction growing among those concerned about the future of our society that such current assumptions about education and where and how it happens need to be radically changed to provide more opportunities for a truly human and humanizing education for everyone.

The two following chapters, then, will discuss some of the chief criticisms now being leveled at our educational "system" and suggestions as to how it might be more or less radically changed. We will concentrate on criticisms and suggestions about schools precisely because they are considered the chief educational agency in our society. (Also, in some places and situations, schools are one agency which administrators, teachers, parents, and citizens generally might be able to affect, especially if they united their efforts.)

It should be kept in mind, however, that our schools are not only a powerful formative agency in our society but also a product of it. We have the kind of schools we deserve. Criticisms of them imply criticisms of the society that produced and fosters them; suggestions for changes in schooling imply correspondingly more or less radical changes in society itself. And, in the developing view, Christians should be working for changes, however radical, that offer real "hope for humanization." [13]

13. *The Hope for Humanization* is the title of a book by John Julian Ryan (New York: Newman Press, 1972).

3
Why Send Children to School?

A CARTOON IN *The New Yorker* for October 16, 1971, shows two small children about to enter an uninviting door in a brick wall on which can be seen the first two letters of "Hill School," with a shadowy glum adult figure and more children inside. The caption reads: "Six more years of this, four years of high school, four more of college, and then a job. How did we ever get into such a mess?"

More and more students and teachers in schools and colleges, and more and more people paying for these institutions through taxes and otherwise, are asking themselves this question (though we may hope that most second-graders don't look so far ahead). Today's rising tide of complaint has made evident how ambivalent we Americans are about formal education for the young. We expect so much from it as the hope for realizing a truly democratic society, and yet we have allowed expectations which are totally opposed to real democracy to dominate what actually happens in most schools and through our whole educational "system." These antihumanizing expectations and their consequences are the subject of this chapter.

Custodial Care

Almost every mother with school-age children finds herself sighing with relief when her children go back to school in September or after the Christmas vacation. Every mother whose children are all in school or grown up remembers how life changed when the youngest finally went to school with the rest. During the six hours or so every day when the children are at school, the school and not the mother is responsible for keeping them out of trouble; she can think about and do other things besides child-minding. Mothers who remember some of the infinite boredom of their own school days may feel a pang at the thought of their lively sons and daughters imprisoned at desks, indoors, on a beautiful September day—but they cannot help feeling relieved, all the same, that other people are responsible for the children for a few hours.

In other words, schools provide "custodial care" for children, leaving their parents free for other jobs or occupations. Most fathers work away from home anyway, and, as more and more mothers have gone to work—out of financial need, interest, or just to get out of the house—this custodial-care purpose of schooling has become increasingly important. How many parents, as things are in our society, would or could have charge of their children all day long, all year round? Allied to this custodial-care function is the high school's added purpose of keeping older adolescents out of the labor market. (This was one of the chief reasons, history suggests, for extending to sixteen the age for compulsory schooling.)

As a result, all adults except teachers are cut off from children and adolescents for the major part of the day, and children and adolescents are cut off from the adult world. The fact that our society has encouraged this segregation out of school as well as by means of schools has led some critics to conclude that Americans really don't like young people; they don't want them around. Whatever truth there may be in this observation, the characteristic work-places for adults in our culture—factories, offices, and laboratories—are certainly not set up to function efficiently with children on hand; nor would it benefit the children to be in them—something not necessarily true of the farms and workshops of other cultures. In any case, the question is worth asking: is such a separation of the young from all adults except teachers for so much of their time really good for anyone, including the teachers?

Still more, this custodial function has nothing to do with the "process of training the knowledge, mind, will, character, etc." —which is the definition of "education" given in Webster's Collegiate Dictionary. In fact, it positively inhibits such training when, because of overcrowding, inadequate facilities, distorted student and teacher attitudes, and other ills afflicting so many schools—and especially those for the nonaffluent—this custodial function becomes primary. The teacher's efforts must be mainly directed to trying to keep the children as quiet as possible at their desks in their classrooms—an occupation for jailers, not teachers.

One of our sons was actually told that this was precisely all that was expected of him when he went as a substitute teacher to a public school in Boston. What made him even unhappier than this assignment, he said, was the attitude of contempt for the children, as not being capable of learning anything anyway, on the part of the principal and the teacher for whom he was to substitute. An even more jailerlike assignment was given to a friend of ours: to take charge of the fourth-grade boys whom their regular teachers couldn't handle. These fifteen children, a few simply slow learners and the rest more or less severely emotionally disturbed, had been relegated to the dingy basement of the school, with no facilities and no equipment. Fortunately, the school was so desperate for someone to take charge of these boys that our friend was able to make his own conditions—one of which was to be allowed to take them outdoors when he wanted to.

In many schools, of course, this custodial-care function is not primary. Nonetheless, it is implicit in our present framework of compulsory schooling for so many hours of so many days of so many years. And it is very evident in the traditional classroom setup, with the teacher up in front and the children in orderly rows at desks, moving only when the bell rings to go in orderly files to another classroom. Many parents unconsciously rely on the school's enforcing this kind of "discipline." They feel incapable of disciplining the children themselves, and count on the school to make the children learn to obey orders and keep quiet. These are, of course, abilities that everyone needs to acquire, but not as ends in themselves—rather, as elements in acquiring and exercising inner-directed discipline to achieve freely chosen goals. To make normally active children stay immobile and quiet for so many hours of the day is not true discipline, but a form of destructive torture. It might be said that many of us survived such training, and that therefore it can't be so very harmful. But how much better persons might we be if our schooling had developed our potentialities for responsible freedom from the first grade on, rather than keeping us in this kind of "order"?

Two questions, then, are being asked by people concerned with renewing education. How can schools and schooling be redesigned to develop rather than to stifle young people's capabilities for responsible freedom? Do children and young people need to spend so much time in formal learning situations in order to develop their potentialities? Might not other kinds of situations also be educational?

The Ladder to Opportunity, Jobs, Status, Success

Another major reason for sending children to school—as no parent needs to be reminded—is that formal education has become the ladder to economic and social opportunity. As is frequently pointed out in TV spots and the like, high-school dropouts find it hard to get any kind of job, college graduates earn many times more income in their lives than nongraduates, while doctors, lawyers, and people with further professional training have still more security and numerous financial and status opportunities open to them. To be accurate, one should rather say, "are *supposed* to have more security, etc.," since at present many Ph.D's are happy to get work as "sanitary engineers"; the top of the educational ladder has turned into a jumping-off place. As a matter of fact, this ladder function mainly works negatively: without such-and-such a diploma or degree you can't get x job; but your possessing it by no means guarantees that you actually do get the job.

This reason for going to school gets through to children very early, but mainly in a destructive form; if you don't succeed in school, you won't succeed anywhere. It doesn't matter whether you really learn anything; what is important is to get the marks to get the diploma to get the job—or, for the children whose parents have more ambitious expectations, to get the marks in school and in the Scholastic Aptitude Tests (SAT) to get into a good college to get the marks to get the degree to get the job or get into a good graduate school. . . .

Of course, the idea that the more education a person has, the better off he will be as a person and the more he will be able to contribute to his society is a sound one *if* it means "the more he is developing and training his knowledge, mind, will, character, etc." Certainly the idealistic promoters of equal and increasing opportunities for formal education for everyone hoped that opportunities for such development were what was being made available in schools and colleges.

But our society has too generally come to take the form for the substance: to accept the amount of time spent in schooling, and the marks and diplomas and degrees gained, as evidences of degrees of educatedness, and then to assess and categorize people's potentialities and to assign them socioeconomic roles and opportunities on this dubious basis.

And it *is* dubious, because the tests given in most schools, such as IQ tests and SAT, are designed to measure a very narrow range of knowledge and abilities:

> Another challenge to the testing profession immediately followed the ETS (Educational Testing Service) meeting with the release of the College Entrance Examination Board's commissioned task force report. It scored the standard Scholastic Aptitude Test *as too narrow and as having a stultifying effect on education.* The panel urged replacing it with tests of various abilities beyond verbal and mathematical skills, including artistic talent, social responsibility, leadership, political skill, information management, motivation, temperament and styles of analysis and synthesis.[1]

Whether such abilities, let alone those of wonder, openness, and the like, can be measured through an "instrument" scored by a computer is a real question. But the recommendations of this task force are at least a heartening sign.

Several very unfortunate results have followed from this now almost worldwide acceptance of the fallacies that amounts of time spent in schools or courses equal education, and that people's potential can be assessed on the basis of how well they have done in school and in mass-administered tests such as the IQ and SAT.

For one thing, children are categorized from their first year in

1. *Behavior Today*, Nov. 9, 1970.

school onward as "bright" or "average" or "slow," and once they have been placed in one or another category, their rating is likely to become a self-fulfilling prophecy. The "slow" children feel themselves failures from the start and their teachers expect them to be, thus increasing manyfold the likelihood of their failing.

A widely reported experiment was carried out by a group of educators who asked a large public school if they might administer a new and special kind of intelligence test to the students, and were allowed to do so. They then went to the teachers in the school and told them which children were going to turn out to be "bloomers," capable of high achievement—their selection being purely a random one and having nothing to do with the results of the test. A year later, the group came back and asked the teachers about these students. Sure enough, the great majority had done much better than previously—yet the only factor in the situation which had changed was the teachers' expectations. This experiment obviously has a message for parents as well as teachers: "Oh, yes, John's our bright boy, but poor Jane just can't study. . . ." Do we, too, type our children by their school achievements and so help to stifle their potentialities?

To make this bad situation worse, many teachers are taught and/or obliged to mark a class's tests on the basis of the "bell-shaped curve"—which means that a graph of the class marks ought to form such a curve, with a few very high marks, a few very low marks, and the rest distributed in the middle range. Similarly, in some schools a student's comparative position in his class, based on averaging his marks for each period or semester, can be very important—as a factor in getting into a "good" college, for instance. As a result, the students in the lower half of the curve or in the lower half of the class come to think of themselves as failures or "low achievers." This can happen even though *all* the class may rate higher, say, on SAT scores than a class in another school. To consider oneself a failure, perhaps from the first grade on, is surely not an attitude conducive to a young person's development.

Still more, the ability to do work that is intrinsically dull, with no immediate interest or reward, is one which middle-class parents, and parents who have hopes of becoming or having their children become middle class, tend to cultivate in their children by their attitudes and expectation, as aristocratic and poor parents do not. Since a great deal of school work as now designed *is* dull—who could possibly enjoy most of the graded "readers" now in use, or the pages and pages of mathematical busy-work laid out in "work books"?—poor children find it much more difficult to keep at it; they do not perceive, as middle-class children have been taught to do, that it may pay off in the long run—if you get the marks.

All this has the further effect of tending to keep the children of the poor permanently in the ranks of the poor, since they will never get the educational credentials needed to get good jobs, let alone to practice the professions. This effect is disastrous enough in our own country where, fortunately, various kinds of efforts are also being made to overcome it. But it is far more disastrous in South America, for instance—so much so that Ivan Illich, for one, believes that any developing country which tries to set up a school system on the European or American model is dooming itself to a hopeless expenditure of money to keep an elect minority of rich and middle-class people rich and middle class, while dooming the great majority of its citizens to continuing ignorance and poverty.[2]

2. Ivan Illich is director of the Center for Intercultural Documentation in Cuernavaca, Mexico. He has expressed his views on education in many different publications and most recently in his book, *De-Schooling Society* (New York: Harper & Row, 1971). This particular aspect of the harmfulness of the present system on developing countries is summed up in an article, "The False Ideology of Schooling," in *Great Issues Today*, published by Encyclopedia Britannica, and reprinted in *Saturday Review*, Oct. 17, 1970.

Thus, here again, the fact that our society has assigned an extrinsic purpose to formal education—to be a ladder to economic opportunity and status—tends to frustrate the achievement of its proper goals. Great numbers of people believe, because of their school records and ratings, that they are incapable of any kind of intellectual development (though there are many kinds besides those rewarded with good marks, as the criticism of the SAT scores reported). Moreover, a large number of those who "make it" to college have either lost all interest in such development or do not believe that college will assist them in it. Not long ago, for example, three professors teaching English in a middle-sized men's college asked their sophomore students who among them would go on to graduate if they could get as good jobs without a college degree as with one. More than two-thirds of the students said that they would pack up and leave as soon as possible.

Moreover, because our society gives top priority to school marks and diplomas, and going to school and doing the homework take so much time, it is practically impossible for children in many situations to discover that they have abilities not required by school work—in music or the fine arts or crafts, for instance—or seriously to cultivate them if they do discover them. One of the girls indicted in the Manson trial, for instance, when asked how she came to join a hippie group in the first place, is reported to have said that there she discovered for the first time that she could make something—dresses, adornments, music, dishes. And she had been to a very "good" high school. True, such a situation is the parents' fault at least as much as the school's. True also that parents who can afford it can pay for music lessons, and that most cities provide various Saturday and summertime art and craft classes in museums and elsewhere. But all these are "extras," whereas opportunities for cultivating such abilities should have at least equal time with "academic" subjects for a person's all-round development. How hungry young people are for music is obvious—often painfully so to middle-aged ears. They teach themselves the guitar; they sing; they listen endlessly to records. But does this not indicate a deep need for an education broader than the "book learning" provided in school, a need which they try to satisfy as best they can?

Thus between the custodial-care and the ladder functions of formal education, it is clear that vast human potentialities are remaining uncultivated in our society, and many people are beginning to ask: what can be done about it?

Socialization

A third reason for sending children to school, and for the existence of our school "system," is to form them as members of a particular society, social class, subculture, religious group, etc., according to some more or less clearly defined model. Private schools, colleges, and universities try (in however vague and grandiose terms) to specify in their catalogues what they intend their ideal graduates to be like (unless the institution is so distinguished that it feels no need for such a description: as the old saying goes, "You can tell a Harvard man, but you can't tell him much"). Where a choice is available, parents try to choose the schools for their children which seem most likely to form them as the parents want them formed, with the kinds of values, knowledge, and skills that the parents want them to possess.

It is, of course, a human necessity that children should go through a process of socialization—that is, of being gradually initiated into the values, norms, and customs of their society, and of acquiring the knowledge and skills needed to contribute to its continuance. We are born dependent on other people, not only for existence and physical survival, but for perceiving reality and responding to it in a human way. Thus "becoming human" necessarily means doing so initially as a member of a particular family culture, religion, and society, with their particular limitations and potentialities.

Moreover, for a family or a culture or a society to survive, its members must share some consensus on values, norms, ways of doing things and tasks to be done—a consensus which is transmitted to growing children and reinforced all through life to the extent to which the person remains under these influences.

But the vital question is: what is the main thrust of this consensus? Is it, as with the dominant modern "civilized" societies, to serve some nonhuman values erected into absolutes: race, nation, technological progress? Or is it directed toward a kind of personal and communal development which tries to foster the widest possible spectrum of human values, to encourage a diversity of life-styles and other options in a climate of mutual respect and appreciation, and which would thus help persons to transcend the limitations of their particular family, group, nationality, culture, and to imagine and work toward a "beyond"?

If it is the first, then the education given in such a society must be mainly what the great Brazilian educator Paulo Freire calls "education for domestication": forming people to accept and carry out some predetermined role without asking any real questions about where they are and where they are going. If it is the second, it is what he calls "education for liberation": enabling and equipping people to stand off from any given situation, to analyze its components, to judge it in terms of more and more ultimate values, to determine how best to change it, and to go to work to do so.[3]

Our American ideals, as expressed in the Declaration of Independence and the Constitution, obviously call for a liberating education in Freire's sense. The values on which the consensus is based that binds us together as a society were intended to be those that make authentic freedom possible and foster it. But the freedom to pursue happiness, that is, to seek the Ultimate,

3. See Paulo Freire, *Pedagogy of the Oppressed* (New York: Herder and Herder, 1970), and his *Cultural Action for Freedom* (Cambridge, Mass.: Harvard Educational Review and Center for the Study of Development and Social Change, 1970).

has always been threatened by forces that would domesticate us in the service of some false god, some inhuman value. And today it seems to have become increasingly clear that, if we are to survive, we must arrive at a consensus in favor of complete domestication (as J. B. Skinner urges in *Beyond Freedom and Dignity*), and implement it thoroughly through every socializing agency—or achieve a consensus on our original American values and try to implement them. The second would seem to be the American and the Christian choice, but unfortunately, as a vast amount of research seems to indicate, the main thrust of most formal schooling in the United States is toward domestication, reinforced by the custodial-care concept and the aim to provide a ladder to economic opportunity and status.

The first proponents of universal schooling realized that an enlightened citizenry, able to control its government, is essential to the healthy working of a democracy: they intended a generally liberating kind of education even though, as we shall see in a later chapter, it had a strong moralistic thrust. Then the immigration of vast and varied ethnic groups seemed to indicate the need for a powerful agent to "Americanize" the children of these immigrants, and the school was the obvious candidate for this task. The school thus gradually became a more and more important means of socializing young Americans, with the family and the Church handing over more and more of what had been their responsibilities to it. But, at the same time, the socializing achieved by the school came more and more to mean inculcating conformity rather than mutually creative freedom. As a result, the main thrust of our present educational system might be summed up in the brief answer given by an immigrant high school boy, whose English was more pungent than politely correct, to a visiting consultant teacher who had urged him to show more initiative: "I make initiative and they give me hell!"

Very naturally, but very unfortunately, Catholic schools in the past have generally had the same thrust. The preconciliar view of life did not encourage Catholics to question any status quo. Moreover, since they were both ethnically and religiously "foreigners" to the dominant Anglo-Saxon Protestant ethos (and also until very recently widely suspected of being agents of the "foreign power" of Rome), they have been eager to show themselves as American as anyone else, and more so. Thus Catholic schools have in general been very effective agents of domestication—their success in enforcing order and inculcating obedience making them the envy of public-school administrators and causing them to seem desirable to many non-Catholic parents.

Universities and colleges should, of course, above all serve as agents of liberation in Freire's sense: the purpose of academic freedom is to ensure that free and freeing enquiry into one or another aspect of reality is not inhibited by any kind of domesticating pressures. The term "liberal arts" originally meant the knowledge and skills proper to a free man (as opposed to a slave), so that he could take his part in conducting the affairs of his city or state wisely, having the leisure to consider and discuss not merely how to get necessary tasks done, but ultimate principles and values. (Incidentally, the Greek word from which "school" is derived means "leisure"; it would be interesting to collect comments on this fact from high school and college students.) Thus a "liberal arts education" should be liberating, in Freire's sense, since it should enable people to judge the way things are (themselves, their schools and colleges, their society and its institutions) by more ultimate principles than those of immediate utility or accepted myths such as the inevitability of "progress," the intrinsic superiority of the "American way of life" over every other, and so on.

Yet somehow, as so many books and articles and reports have brought out in the last few years, our colleges and universities have too generally been failing to provide a truly liberal and liberating education. They have been training future businessmen, financiers, lawyers, doctors, social scientists, engineers, teachers, etc., to fit into predetermined slots in society—more subtly, perhaps, but just as effectively as ghetto schools have been training people to be able to qualify only for unskilled labor.

One reason why this domesticating thrust of college and university education has only recently begun to be recognized is the long-accepted myth of the "scientist" as engaged in pursuing objective, "value-free" truths, in a social, moral, and political vacuum, and training students to do the same—an ideal which, it has been felt for many decades, all other disciplines should be trying to emulate as best they could. This myth is now being seen to have been a false one. The "scientist's" view of reality is as conditioned by his own psychology, socialization, and life experience as is anybody else's. Moreover, what a scientist chooses to investigate already implies a value judgment, as does where he goes to get funding and what he allows to be done with his discoveries. But it is a dangerous myth, since it means that scientists and technologists too generally have not been making conscious and considered value judgments or allowances for their own biases, with the result that in many cases they have allowed themselves to be used for enslaving and dehumanizing purposes.

In the same way, many people in the behavioral or social sciences are now realizing that, while these new disciplines were intended to be as objective and value-free as the physical sciences were supposed to be, instead they have generally been taking conformist, white, middle-class Americans and their social structures as the norm by which to judge desirable or undesirable behavior, social trends, etc.[4] And, as the clamor for women's liberation, Black studies, and Third World courses of all kinds has been bringing out, however onesidedly, the same has been true to a greater or less degree of all disciplines, including theology.

4. See, for example, Seymour L. Halleck, M.D., *The Politics of Therapy* (New York: Science House, 1971). Also the first chapter in Charles Hampden-Turner's book, *Radical Man*, *op. cit.*, in which he discusses "the borrowed toolbox" of the physical sciences which the social sciences have been using, and the whole concept of "value-free science."

It is, of course, against these dehumanizing purposes of schooling that young people have been mainly protesting—however confused their motivations in many cases and however ill-advised some of their actions may have been. For high-schoolers to concentrate a great deal of energy on gaining the right to dress and wear their hair as they wish, for instance, can easily be interpreted as an indication that they are not very serious about learning anything. On the other hand, the angry reactions of many parents and administrators to such a proposal makes it just as easy to suspect that they do not take real education very seriously either; what they are interested in is conformity to their norms.

What *is* distressing about much recent protesting is that the students' education has equipped so few of them to analyze intelligently and carefully what they believe to be a domesticating, unfree situation, the values at stake, the obstacles to be overcome and the resources available, and to plan and execute some course of action that has a reasonable chance of succeeding. This is all the sadder because courses in many schools (and religion classes), as well as the daily news on TV and elsewhere, dramatically bring home to them the ills of our society but leave them feeling helpless to do anything to improve it. As a result, a great many "cop out," with the help of various—and sometimes dangerous—avenues of private escape, or return to conformism.

We adults, of course, are all too generally not in much better case; in many areas of our lives we have learned that "I make initiative and they give me hell." But, happily, some hopeful trends can be discerned of people arousing themselves from apathy and acceptance of "the way things are" to try to do something to improve them: Common Cause, for instance; the Committee for a More Effective Senate; Cesar Chavez's movement; welfare mothers' organizations.

At the same time, many experiments are being carried on and proposals made for a more or less radical change of our present educational "system." The following chapter presents some of these experiments and proposals which may offer promising possibilities for education for liberation, a truly human and humanizing education.

4
What Kinds of Education Do We Want?

A HUNGARIAN FRIEND of ours was doing very well in mastering Russian until he tackled the verbs. Then, even though his instructor was an attractive woman whom he greatly admired, he gave up, because, he said, "I feel like a very small ant lost in a tremendous forest." Anyone feels much the same way who tries to penetrate today's jungle of educational theories and methods, especially when they are explained in "educationese"— a more difficult and much less beautiful language than Russian. Happily, however, many spokesmen for more human kinds of education, among them Holt, Silberman, and Glasser,[1] write

1. John Holt, *How Children Fail; How Children Learn; The Under-achieving School,* and his most recent, *What Do I Do Monday?* (New York: E. P. Dutton, 1970). Charles E. Silberman, *Crisis in the Classroom: The Remaking of American Education* (New York: Random House, 1970). William Glasser, M.D., *Schools without Failure* (New York: Harper & Row, 1969).

clear English that anyone can understand. In this chapter I will try to present some general lines along which reformers and innovators are working, and what some schools or groups are doing, in their efforts to replace the anti-educational functions just discussed. This survey will necessarily broaden out from the school to the community and its various actual or potential educational agencies, for two trends which might either complement or conflict with one another seem to be at work: to improve and broaden the scope of what happens in schools, and to aim toward a lesser amount of formal education for the young, or even the complete deschooling of our society.

As opposed to the *custodial-care function* and its effects, a more humanizing education would:

1. Foster respect for the unique dignity and potentialities of each person
2. Help people develop in the responsible use of freedom
3. Make it possible for and encourage people of different ages and abilities to learn together and teach one another
4. Help people to learn how to learn in many different situations
5. Reintegrate "learning" with "life"

These aims call for a completely different environment from that of the usual school—different in the way space and equipment and time are used, different in the way in which persons relate to one another.

The trend toward "open" schools and classrooms is obviously in this direction. Instead of uniform boxlike rooms, with the teacher's desk up front and the students' desks fixed in neat rows, the given space is arranged so as to allow for a variety of learning places for different purposes. There might be, for example, a reading place with books and magazines and comfortable chairs (and a rug for youngsters who like reading on the floor). There might be a music place, appropriately furnished and soundproofed. And a dancing place, a games place, a mathematics place, and so on. Each area would have its own rules appropriate to the kind of learning going on in it.[2]

In such a school, students are free to choose between different kinds of learning, with reasonable limitations on how often they can move from one to the other, and to plan and carry out their own projects, individually or in groups. Such schools are becoming quite common in England on the lower levels, and the movement toward them is beginning to spread to the higher ones.[3] They are being experimented with in many places in America in both public and private systems.

The situation in such an open school clearly calls for a relationship between the teachers and the students quite different from the traditional one of order-keeper and information-giver to passive recipients. The teacher's function becomes that of a facilitator and resource person, helping the students to channel their interests and to use the available resources, suggesting possibilities—and to "teach" in the traditional sense only when called upon to do so. To carry out these roles, the teacher must develop a considerable degree of empathy with the students —and also with the other teachers, who have to cooperate as a team in a very flexible way.

People who have visited such schools which are working well, with teachers who enjoy this kind of "coaching" and are competent at it, say that no one used to the traditional kind of school can imagine how alive, happy, and productive this kind of education can be. (Incidentally, the children *do* learn to read and write and often much more quickly than in the traditional type of schooling.[4])

But with teachers untrained in and unhappy with an open

2. See Gerard A. Pottebaum, "A Place to Learn, a Place to Pray," *The Living Light*, vol. 8, no. 4 (Winter, 1970–71), p. 63.

3. See the chapter, "The Case of the New English Primary Schools" in Silberman, *Crisis in the Classroom.* Also Joseph Featherstone, "Open Schools, the British and Us," *The New Republic*, Sept. 11, 1971, and "Tempering the Open School Fad," *ibid.*, Sept. 25, 1971.

4. See, for example, John Holt, *What Do I Do Monday?*

situation, pure chaos results. To make the change in attitude and to acquire the skills needed for this kind of open educating is not easy for many teachers long accustomed to a more traditional type. Where such schools are successful, the teachers have usually been given considerable retraining to help them make the transition.[5] And, too, children used to two, three, or four—let alone eight—years of traditional schooling need help in adjusting to such a new situation, to realize that they are responsible for their own learning, and coresponsible with their fellow students and the teachers for the school and its resources.

Thus it serves no useful purpose to spend large sums building an open school which is simply an empty place. The teachers need to learn how to use this space creatively, and so do the students; consideration must be given to the new opportunities it offers to both. (On the other hand, creative people who want to try this kind of teaching—and are allowed to do so—can rearrange even a traditional classroom, if the desks are not bolted to the floor, as a suitable environment for different kinds of learning, by the use of space-dividers, posters and slides, varied materials, and so on.[6])

An open school could have the further advantage of making it not only possible but natural for students of different ages to teach one another—something also being done in more traditional situations with great benefit. (In this respect, as in some others, an open school is not so different from the one-room little red schoolhouse at its best.) It also makes it easier to invite adults other than teachers to come into one or another

5. See the second Featherstone article referred to in footnote 3, above, also the final chapter, "The Education of Educators" in Silberman, *Crisis in the Classroom.*

6. The Tree House Learning Environment, an integrated modular system of space-arrangers, rear projection screens, seating blocks and graphics, designed to enrich the aesthetic quality of learning places and to extend the versatility of existing facilities and in economizing in the construction of new buildings, is being used in a wide variety of situations. For information, write The Tree House, P. O. Box 2243, Kettering, Ohio 45429.

learning situation as resource persons, paraprofessionals, or volunteers, thus beginning to break down the wall between the school and the local community, the school and the wider adult community.

A further development of the open school might, then, be its becoming a community learning center, offering a variety of opportunities to people of all ages, to which people of all ages could contribute in different ways.

Along the same lines, but on a much vaster scale, are the "educational parks" already designed for some communities with all the resources that modern technology can put at the service of education. The apotheosis of such a park, in which the adults as well as the children of the year 2001 spend much of their abundant leisure time, is described in *Education and Ecstasy*.[7] Computers to teach the "basics" in the most efficient way, simulated cultures of other times and places, games, history acted out—educational ecstasy indeed.

On the other hand, some people are suggesting that, rather than constructing elaborate schools or educational "parks," why not have young people go where the resources for different kinds of learning already exist? Thus, for example, the much-written-up Parkway School in Philadelphia has only a small administrative headquarters, from which the students go to learn in libraries, museums, concert halls, courthouses, offices, workshops, and factories. Or again, a private high school in the southwest sends students away to different environments of their own choice for a semester—a Navajo reservation, a Mormon or Buddhist community . . . .

One can imagine various developments of this idea. Why shouldn't young people with special talents and interests be allowed to cultivate them for a considerable part of the present "school day"? For example, the Community School of the Arts in New York City's Harlem provides professional training in

7. George B. Leonard, *Education and Ecstasy* (New York: Delacorte Press, 1968), chap. 8, "Visiting Day, 2001 A.D.," pp. 139 ff.

the dramatic and musical arts for underprivileged children and young people. But, as things are now, they can attend it only after school, on weekends, and during vacations. How much more might their talents be developed if they could spend school time at it? Some public and private schools are, in fact, already beginning to revise their curriculum along such lines, not only by providing new courses, or new possibilities of combining specialties (e.g., "shop" and higher mathematics), but also by allowing students to pursue genuine interests at other institutions and in working situations.

Or again, there are many tasks in every community, especially in the line of personal services, which young people could carry out as one aspect of their education for a certain amount of time each week in helping care for the isolated elderly, making some aspect of their environment more livable in some way, and so on as, in some communities, high school students can volunteer to work in hospitals—but, as things mainly are, only in out-of-school time.

Perhaps the most radical proposal for "deschooling" our society is that made by Ivan Illich. Rather than having any schools, each city would have one or several centers of information about all the available resources such as libraries, museums, theaters, movies, lectures, etc. Another center would provide the names of anyone in the community who was competent and willing to teach a skill—from carpentry and plumbing to ballet dancing or handling a foreign language—and match up the people who wanted to learn these skills with those who offered to teach them. Still another center would provide the same service for people who wanted to teach or learn in a master/disciple personal relationship. And a fourth kind of center would be staffed with professional "educators" who would help adults, young people, and parents with their children, to make the best use of all these services for their particular needs and interests. Everyone would receive at birth a given quantity of educational vouchers, which could be spent at any time in his life, and people could be full- or part-time paid "teachers" in one or other of the above-mentioned capacities.[8]

The great advantage, it seems to me, of the deschooling approach in general over the "educational park" one is that it does not require expensive buildings and equipment, though it could use them if they were available. It offers less temptation to allow technological progress and the commercialism that feeds on it to dictate to education. It puts people and human resources first. Further, it can more easily give priority to firsthand experiences of persons and things and situations, to personal activity and creativity, over the secondhand experiences that the media can provide in such abundance in schools as well as homes. Of course, such secondhand experiences—like those provided by reading—can widen and deepen people's firsthand experiences. But it cannot substitute for them, unless we want to become more and more a society of passive TV watchers and button-pushers at the mercy of conscious and unconscious manipulators.

Perhaps a combination of the open school and the deschooling approaches would be viable, in some places at least, in the not too distant future, through a community center which would provide an open school and also, for adolescents and adults, the kinds of services Illich suggests. Thus the young children could be cared for in a noncustodial fashion, and gradually given wider opportunities outside the school as they matured.

As opposed to the ladder-and-labeling functions, a more humanizing education would:

1. Rely on and encourage people's intrinsic motivations for learning: interest, delight, skillful action, service of others

8. See Ivan Illich, "The Alternative to Schooling," *Saturday Review,* June 19, 1971, pp. 44 ff.

2. Encourage cooperation rather than competition
3. Help people cultivate a wide range of abilities and interests rather than forcing them to acquire a predetermined body of knowledge and skills at a predetermined pace
4. Put the well-being and development of persons ahead of "efficiency"

Such educational aims challenge several long-standing assumptions, the first being that people, children especially, don't want to learn and must be forced to do so by some compulsion, or by some motivation that has nothing to do with learning—winning a reward or the hope of making money. This assumption is simply untrue. Small children, as several writers have recently pointed out, learn the very complex skills of walking and talking because they want to get around, imitate their elders, and communicate; nobody needs to force or bribe normal children to learn, though they may encourage and help them.

Again, small children are naturally curious: every mother knows the "Why?" stage of development, and the stage at which she is continually trying to keep the child from getting into things and situations that might harm him. And small children are naturally creative and active; they want to be doing things and making things.

Moreover, learning for interest or pleasure is not limited to children. Young people and adults do not have to be forced to acquire incredible amounts of information about kinds of cars, or their favorite sport, or current records, or to study "How to" books about doing something they are interested in and then practice what the books tell them.

Creative educators, therefore, who work with the conviction that children want to learn unless their curiosity is stifled or starved, try to nourish children's normal interests and to open to them new possibilities of finding out about reality from many aspects and learning how to deal with it. For example, rather than the "Dick and Jane" approach to reading, a child might be asked to name something he especially likes or dislikes, and then asked if he would want to see the word written out. He might trace the letters and go on to write them himself, and so day by day compose his own word list and share it with other children. Or he might be shown how to measure people or things (his own and the other children's height, for instance, or the length of the whole room and of parts of it), and thus begin to gain basic mathematical skills.[9]

Another assumption challenged by this approach is that learning ought to be painful rather than enjoyable. How are children to learn discipline unless they are made to work hard and do things they don't like doing? Or, as the nineteenth-century humorist Peter Finley Dunne has his Irish-American Misther Dooley put it: "Any subject's a good subject pervided the shtoodent don't like it."

Of course, learning to do anything well, from playing the guitar to speaking French, from skating to philosophizing, sooner or later does require a great deal of hard work, even drudgery. But the aim of this approach is to make it evident to the student that the hard work is worth it for the goal he wants to attain. Nobody forces a professional writer to revise and throw away and revise again; he imposes such discipline on himself in order to turn out a piece of work that will come somewhere near to saying what he wants to say. Nobody forces musicians or champion athletes to practice for many hours. This approach to learning tries to communicate such a "professional" attitude to students, whether about cooking, or putting on a play, or communicating in a foreign language.

This means that acquiring information about this or that area of human knowledge is understood to be not an end in itself, but one aspect of cultivating an ability. Thus if a parent asks a child, "What did you learn in school today?" he should look for a "How to" kind of answer: how to add two columns,

9. See Holt, *What Do I Do Monday?*

how to read a road map, and not a "that" answer: that Boston is the capital of Massachusetts.

In other words, people at any age need to be encouraged to become read*ers* and writ*ers*, rather than "learning" reading or writing; they should be helped to philosophize and think historically, rather than "taking" philosophy or history (like a pill). Above all, they should learn how to learn, as Margaret Mead puts it,[10] so that they can and want to go on cultivating their abilities all their lives.

Another assumption hidden in the ladder-and-labeling idea of education is that since people, and particularly children, are naturally hoggish, their hoggishness might as well be utilized as a motivation to learn: to beat other people, now by good marks, and in the future by better jobs than "dummies" can obtain. Thus each student is considered a monad, an isolated unit, put in school primarily to advance his own interests as best he can. This attitude is enforced by the whole grade system (to be "normal" a child should be in such a grade at such an age) and by the importance given to marks and class rank in many college-admission policies. The more humanizing education represented by the open school, on the contrary, tries to foster each person's sense of his individual worth and his abilities to work with and for other persons in different kinds of groups.

One step in this direction is the "ungraded" school, in which a child may belong to one group for reading, a different one for mathematics, and so on. Another step is abolishing of marks in favor of a simple pass/fail, and still another a teacher evaluation of each student at certain intervals and one by the student himself, the two to be compared and discussed by both.

Happily, some colleges and universities are going along with this trend. Silberman said, in an interview on television's "Today" show in April, 1971, that one high school which was being reorganized along these lines wrote to a considerable

10. In her book, *Culture and Commitment* (Garden City, N.Y.: Doubleday, 1970).

number of representative colleges asking whether they would accept such evaluations in considering admissions instead of the usual records. All but three said, "Yes," and one of those three explained that their computer would have to be reprogrammed to handle the omission of class rank, but that this would be done by the following year.

Of course, if this trend is to grow, it will involve setting up new criteria for judging people's qualifications for graduate and professional schools, for practicing professions, for taking jobs and positions of all kinds. These criteria will have to be developed on the basis of people's abilities, their competence, wherever or however acquired, and their potentialities for increasing and adding to it, rather than whether or not they have "graduated" from one or another kind of institution. It will also involve the public's growing acceptance of these new criteria.

But, after all, nobody asks a star baseball player about his school record; nobody cares whether a comedian or an actor went to college or not, so long as he "does his thing" well; nobody asks the man who is going to repair his car if he has a high school diploma. Why, then, should one need a college degree to get a clerk's job in a bank? Or why should someone who can show that he knows how to write good clear English and that he can develop this ability in others have to possess, not only a college degree, but also specified courses in "education" before he can be allowed to teach in a high school?

Such questions, of course, bring up the whole complex problem of professionalism, an area about which teachers in particular are most understandably very sensitive. The way in which American society generally has treated its teachers throughout our history—demanding so much and giving so little—certainly more than explains this sensitivity and the many tensions to which it gives rise. For example:

In 1967 the southern section of the California Teachers' Association queried many of its members to find out how they fared in terms of personal freedom. A number of respondents, particularly from low-population areas, had complaints. "In my opinion," said a Bonsall teacher, "the private life of a teacher is about as private as a fishbowl if he lives and teaches in a small district." As a Palm Springs teacher wrote the CTA, "What I do, what I say and how I act are always subject to public scrutiny. Teachers affect the community too much for it to be otherwise. . . ." [11]

But also:

Wry comment heard around well-to-do suburban neighborhoods: "You can always tell the difference between the teachers' and the students' parking lots. The students' lot is the one with all the new cars in it." [12]

Thus it is no wonder that teachers' associations are so generally preoccupied with questions of salaries, qualifications for better positions, and so on, which may have very little to do with competence in teaching or administration. Yet the present system, not only in teaching but in every profession which has standardized its qualifications by quantity of courses taken and diplomas or degrees gained, does not encourage good teaching or good medical care or good anything else. The problem is how to assess competence, or a person's ability to gain competence, in a less inhuman and mechanical way, by demonstrated motivation and capability rather than by amounts of time spent in educational institutions and degrees gained.

For example, an article in the education section of *Newsweek* (Jan. 10, 1972, p. 65) entitled "Bucking the System" describes a program set up three years previous by Dr. Gary Huber at Boston City Hospital, the purpose of which is "to expose interested young people to medical procedures and give them posi-

11. Myron Brenton, *What's Happened to Teacher?* (New York: Coward McCann, Inc., 1970), p. 79.
12. *Ibid.*, p. 94.

tions of genuine responsibility in a research laboratory . . . ."
Huber, as a one-man screening board, looks for motivation, not
academic credentials, in the dozen or more teen-agers who
volunteer for work in his laboratory (the Channing Laboratory
for Infectious Diseases) each year. One of his volunteers,
Hunter Nicholas, though he went through the stifling ghetto
school described by Jonathan Kozol in *Death at an Early Age,*
became at the age of 18 the first pre-college student to present
an original paper to the forty members of the American Federa-
tion for Clinical Research. In the meantime, to give him help
in reading and understanding medical terminology, Huber and
his associates arranged for his enrollment at the Palfrey Street
(private) school where, within two years, he was "unanimously
elected to the school's board of trustees and was teaching classes
in freshman algebra and black literature." This is a story of individual achievement but also suggests a possible breakthrough in
assessing and cultivating persons' human potential and offering
them opportunities to exercise it irrespective of their accredited
"formal" education.

One encouraging trend in this direction is the use of paraprofessionals and volunteers in education and other service professions, selected on the basis of their qualifications other than
academic, and given whatever further training is really needed
to do the job. In some places, for example, women whose mar-
riages seem to be stable and happy, and whose children are
grown, are asked to take some training in marriage counseling
and then to act as marriage counselors, under the direction of a
professional, for people with less-than-acute problems. Such
women would probably be counseling informally in any case:
the training and support simply gives them additional competence and confidence—and those they counsel a sense of
security—while widening their scope of operation.

This example, then, illustrates the possibility that professional
educators might increasingly involve many members of the community in various kinds of educational efforts, and these mem-

bers might discover themselves to be "educators" and also "professionals" in the wide and deep sense of commitment to offer skillful service of a particular kind.

With the amount of leisure prophesied for people in non-professional jobs and occupations, and the obvious and growing need for human services of every kind—most of which are in the widest sense "educational"—can we afford to retain the present educational ladder as the only means of access to rendering many of these services in an accredited framework? Might it not fructify many professions if some proportion of their members had been trained in other than an "orthodox" fashion? These are large questions and beyond the scope of this book, except as they indicate the intimate relationship between improving education and improving society. If we are concerned with developing a liberating education, in Freire's sense, we must be concerned with developing a liberating society also. Would young people brought up to authentic and responsible freedom fit into our present society? Can we bring them up to become sufficiently free and responsible to take over the work of transforming our society into one which favors these qualities rather than their opposites for the majority of mankind?

Thus the various issues that we have been discussing in these two chapters are all connected more or less directly with the central question: should the thrust of all our educational agencies, actual and potential, be toward domesticating people or liberating them? Many critics of humankind believe, with the Grand Inquisitor in Dostoevski's *The Brothers Karamazov*, that the vast majority of people really do not want freedom; they are afraid of it. But no society as yet has made a consistent effort to educate all of its citizens for this kind of freedom, for humanness in the sense described earlier. We simply do not know what such a "socializing" process would bring about. In any case, it seems clear that Christians must work for a liberating education. God himself does not force us to become what he wants us to be: who, then, are men to force other men into any kind or arrangement of "little boxes"?

This question is becoming increasingly urgent as social scientists claim to know more and more about human behavior, and certainly do know more and more about how to influence it effectively. J. B. Skinner for example, claims that we already have the means to develop a "technology of behavior" which would "arrange environments in which specific consequences are contingent upon behavior" and so produce a peaceful and happy Utopia, and that this, as was said earlier, is the only means to human survival.[13]

Most of us would agree with the reviewer in the October issue of *Psychology Today* who said that the realization of Skinner's Utopia would seem to him rather "a preview of hell." Yet we are not going to avoid destruction or improve present situations by ignoring the reasonably well-proved discoveries about human behavior and learning, as well as the techniques of influencing them. We need, rather, to learn to discriminate between techniques which are domesticating and those which are liberating, and to use the liberating ones as skillfully as we can.

Except for the alterations in human behavior possible through chemical or electrical or other direct physical interference with the human organism, there is actually no great mystery about any of these techniques. They are refinements and conscious applications, given scientific-sounding names, of what we do to and for one another in daily living. A mother who spanks her small child who has just run across the street without looking for oncoming cars is practicing "behavioral modification." A hostess who arranges the furniture and lighting, provides appropriate food and drinks, and sees to it that her guests have opportunities to talk with the fellow guests most likely to interest them is "structuring the environment." But she may be doing so for a liberating purpose—just to give her friends a

13. See his book, *Beyond Freedom and Dignity* (New York: Alfred A. Knopf, 1971).

happy evening and a chance to meet some new friends. Or she may be doing it for a domesticating one: for example, to put one of the guests in a position where he is obliged or might be more easily persuaded to do her husband a favor. In fact, we usually "structure environments"—which include the people as well as the physical setting—out of very mixed motives. But we need to realize that this is what we are doing whenever we attempt to influence people by ways other than direct argument or persuasion.

In cultivating discrimination about all forms of attempted behavioral modification in the widest sense, it might be helpful, then, to examine the ways in which we structure situations to influence people, and those in which we find that we have been influenced. Are we trying to domesticate or liberate; are we allowing ourselves to be domesticated or liberated? (How do certain TV ads affect us, for instance, or political speeches?)

Thus both existing and new forms and methods of education, in schools and elsewhere, need to be critically examined to ascertain whether they are truly liberating or not, in the concrete circumstances and with the actual persons involved in them. Some Head-Start programs, for instance, and also the widely acclaimed TV program "Sesame Street," have been severely criticized as tending to domesticate children to white middle-class norms of abilities and achievements rather than to liberate them to develop as individuals.

The same critical evaluation is called for with regard to the rapidly multiplying programs which directly aim to help people in one way or another to become more complete personalities, to relate better to others and to the cosmos. "Becoming a Person" programs for children are being introduced under various titles in schools and in religion classes.[14] Encounter-type weekends for young people are available in many settings, while high schools

14. *Becoming a Person* is the title of a complete program for grade schools published by Benziger Bros., San Francisco, with students' texts, teachers' guides, and notes for parents for each grade.

are beginning to offer psychology courses and group counseling. For adults, there is a bewildering variety of sensitivity-training sessions, encounter groups of all shapes and sizes, etc. None can be a universal panacea; some may be very helpful to some kinds of people and extremely harmful to others.

But certainly a basic criterion must be whether or not a given method or program is designed and carried out so as to help people ultimately to take over this aspect of developing their personhood or their abilities themselves. If not, it will be enslaving rather than truly liberating. For example, one of the most promising methods of educating people to begin to free themselves from oppressive socioeconomic situations has been worked out by Paulo Freire and widely tested in South America. Its purpose is, in the process of teaching illiterate peasants to read and write, to help them to an awareness of the various aspects of their situation, so that they can stand outside it and consider what—however little—can be done to remedy it. This aid is offered by a team of people with various competencies in sociology, psychology, economics, and so on, who come and live in a village and discover the people's key concerns, and what symbols and words best express them. Thus, beginning with these words, their progress in literacy becomes at the same time a progress in analyzing their situation, taking some action to improve it, and then reflecting on the new situation brought about by the action.[15] (The reader will note the similarity between this method and the action/reflection method of religious education in Chapter 2. Again, Babin's definition of catechesis, quoted earlier, as "the act by which a group gains awareness, in the light of the Gospel, of the process of the total development of mankind in which it is called to take part," is a Christian development of Freire's ideas.[16])

15. See Miriam Clasby, "Education as a Tool for Humanization and the Work of Paulo Freire," *The Living Light*, vol. 8, no. 1 (Spring, 1971), pp. 48 ff. Also, see Freire's own books cited in chap. 3, footnote 3.
16. In the course of this article, Babin describes his first meeting with

Many other methods are being initiated and adapted more and more widely to help people learn how to educate themselves and one another, to free themselves and one another. "Participatory training," for instance, helps a group discover how to plan a course of action for themselves.[17] A group of teachers might call for such training, for example, in a situation where they were free to plan a flexible kind of curriculum to suit their students' needs and their own competencies, rather than using one mandated by some higher authority and ready-made with texts and teachers' guides. The same kind of training could be used by groups with purposes as diverse as those of parish councils and of a group of adolescents planning a dance.

Even broader approaches, which we will discuss in the final chapter, aim to make a whole community aware of its own resources and able to act positively and consciously as a many-sided education enterprise. Saul Alinsky's work is along these lines, for example, as is that of Kenneth D. Benne.[18]

Which of these methods and trends an individual or a group can initiate or encourage depends, of course, entirely on the situation. But that, as citizens and as Christians, we should be on the alert for liberating approaches and methods and do what we can to assist them, in schools and elsewhere, there can be no doubt at all. This would seem to be the only way of working toward a nonviolent transformation of our society into a more human and humanizing one.

Freire, who began by saying to him, "I don't like catechesis. It is a kind of way of enslaving people. . . ." But after Babin had presented his definition of catechesis, Freire said, "If that's what it is, I'm for it." (*op. cit.*, pp. 62, 72).

17. See Charles C. McDonald, "Participation Training: An Experiment for Teachers in Louisville CCD," *The Living Light*, vol. 7, no. 4 (Winter, 1970), pp. 79 ff. For information about this training write: Bureau of Studies in Adult Education, 309 South Highland Ave., Bloomington, Ind. 47401.

18. See Kenneth D. Benne, *Education in the Quest for Identity and Community* (Columbus: Ohio State University Press, 1962).

Freire's educational work is primarily to help people liberate themselves in the socioeconomic dimension, which also includes a psychological liberation from feeling helpless in the face of "the system." But we all also need to be continually freed from our selfishness and self-centeredness, free to grow as loving, human persons, free to take part in the whole task of human liberation and development. And we need to be continually liberated from our imprisonment in the surface here-and-nowness of our lives—to recognize and welcome the Ultimate. This liberation would seem in one sense to be the precondition of the other two: if we did not recognize some Beyond to our present situation, how could we imagine changing this situation?

This sense of a norm beyond our experience on the basis of which we can say, "This is better, or truer, or more beautiful than that," may be taken, if not as a "proof" of God's existence, at least a "signal of transcendence." In any case, it is certainly closely connected with the question of what basic values people are to live by, and with the question of their basic attitude toward the Ultimate, their "religion" in the widest sense. In a truly pluralistic and free society, particular values and a particular religion cannot be imposed; they must be freely chosen. But the possibility of doing so can and must be opened out to people.

Most cultures in the past, and many persons today, see the question quite differently, considering adherence to their particular set of religious beliefs and practices as the precondition and sanction for acting "rightly," that is, according to the values and norms consequent on these beliefs. These two views obviously produce quite different ideas as to the relationship between religion and education. How the newer view developed from the old, the possibilities of implementing it as a liberating aspect of American education, and the questions it raises for the education of American Catholics are the subject of the next chapter.

5
Education about Religion and Values

THE ASSUMPTION THAT a young person's upbringing should condition him to accept unquestioningly certain religious beliefs and practices, and the values which these sanction and foster, is of course not limited to preconciliar-minded Roman Catholics. Many parents of all faiths accept this goal, just as innumerable young people are rebelling against it. In fact, this assumption has been taken for granted in most societies up to very recent times and, in those in which some kind of more or less formal education was provided, it was intended to assist this process. Even in the late Roman Empire, in which a vast variety of religious beliefs and philosophies were tolerated, Christians complained that the available "higher education," based as it was on the study of Greek classical writings, inculcated pagan beliefs and values rather than Christian ones, and that Christians must learn to distinguish the good in this education from the poison.

During and after the collapse of the Roman Empire and its various educational agencies, the Church took on the work of "formal" education primarily for the sake of its own needs. Future bishops and priests must be able to read, and to interpret what they read, in order to celebrate the liturgy and to hand on and develop Christian teaching. Monks and nuns had to be able to read the Scriptures in order to meditate on them, and to write in order to multiply copies of the Scriptures and to hand on and develop Christian thought and spirituality.

Thus the major episcopal centers and monasteries became centers of education in a more or less formalized sense, while parish priests were urged from time to time to gather promising boys around them and instruct them in reading and writing, as well as in basic prayers and teachings, as a remote preparation for clerical life. While, later on, the great university centers discovered the notion of "academic freedom" and broke away from direct episcopal control, the authorities of the Church generally felt themselves in charge of formal education as of the whole culture and life-style of Christians.

This centuries-long history helps to explain the strenuous efforts of the Catholic Church in more recent times, through the reformation and the Enlightenment, to cling to its right to conduct schools and other educational institutions at least for its own members, even though it could no longer control all education. But Protestants retained the same mentality: the idea, prevalent in Europe for a time after the Reformation, that everyone in a region should have the same religion as its ruler, *cujus regio eius religio*, shows the same conviction that religion and culture and, consequently, education, should all be prescribed as one whole, from above.

The primary purpose of schooling, therefore, for a very long time has been assumed to be formation in one or another specific religio-cultural pattern. Thus, in our own country, the first schools in New England communities indoctrinated children in a particular form of Protestantism. Similarly, the first colleges were designed primarily as seminaries to educate the ministers of one or another Protestant body, as the first Catholic colleges were meant primarily to be seminaries for training priests.

What is known as the Sunday school movement in the history of early America seems to have been a first step toward separating "general" education from indoctrination into the beliefs, practices, and values of a particular form of Protestantism. As it reached this country from England, it was basically a lay movement and not tied to any formal denominational control. The obvious advantage of this movement in a pioneer society was to provide worship services and basic Christian teachings, with at least the rudiments of the "3 R's," to scattered families originally of different denominations. But, some authorities believe, it also prepared the dominant Protestant American public to accept the idea of a basically "Christian education" which would not attempt to teach the particular beliefs of one or another denomination.[1]

Thus when Horace Mann and others began to promote the idea of public weekday schools for all children, inculcating what they understood to be basic Christian teachings and values and leaving the work of inculcating specific doctrines to each church body on Sundays, this concept did not seem as revolutionary as it turned out later to have been. For comparatively few people at that time, in the middle of the nineteenth century, could have dreamed of a "secular" education in the sense that we have come to understand it, that is, one explicitly ignoring *any* religious beliefs.

But this first kind of public education, however acceptable to

1. See William Bean Kennedy, *The Shaping of Protestant Education* (New York: Association Press, 1966), quoted by John F. Murphy, "American Education With and Without Religion," *The Living Light*, vol. 7, no. 3 (Fall, 1970); the Murphy article gives an overview of this whole development.

the majority of Protestants, was by no means acceptable to Catholics, precisely because it was not only Protestant but sometimes positively anti-Catholic and inculcated a strongly Protestant mentality and morality. As Henry Steele Commager says in his introduction to the paperback reprint of the 1879 edition of McGuffey's A *Fifth Eclectic Reader:*

> Certainly, what is most impressive in the McGuffey Readers is the morality. . . . What was the nature of the morality that permeated the Readers? It was deeply religious, and in those mid-century years, in America, religion meant Protestant Christianity. More, it was a Christianity closer to Puritanism than to that Unitarianism which was even then making its way out of New England and into the Ohio country.

Consequently, after various attempts at compromises, the Catholic Church in this country committed itself to establishing schools which would form children as good American *Catholics,* as the only alternative to letting them be formed as good American Protestants.

But, beginning early in our own century, this strongly religious Protestant orientation of the public schools gradually changed to a secular one, in the sense that, increasingly, as has often been said, "God was left out of the picture." The only solution to the dilemma: what should be the ultimate thrust of public schooling in a religiously pluralistic society, and one in which an increasing number do not belong to any established religion? seemed to be an education which ignored religion entirely. Its effort was, rather, to inculcate largely unarticulated "American" values which, some say, make up "the religion of democracy." [2] Thus "godless" public schools came to seem, to

2. See the very interesting chapter, "Civil Religion in America," in Robert Bellah, *Beyond Belief* (New York: Harper & Row, 1970), which begins: "While some have argued that Christianity is the national faith, and others that church and synagogue celebrate only the generalized religion of the American Way of Life, few have realized that there actually exists alongside of and rather clearly differentiated from the churches an

most Catholics, the only alternative to Catholic schools.

To many people, the Supreme Court decision of 1962 in the Engel Case, striking down a state-sponsored program of non-denominational prayer in the public schools of New York State, seemed to mark a final stage in this process of "secularization," a forcing of "godlessness" on children whether their parents wanted it or not. But this was by no means the intention of the Court in this or any other of its decisions about the relationship of religion to public education. What it has declared unconstitutional in public schools are practices which might tend to inculcate one or another form of religion. It has never said that the name of God cannot even be mentioned in a public school. In fact, in the 1963 Schempp Case, on the constitutionality of Bible-reading exercises in public schools, Justice Goldberg said, ". . . the Court would recognize the propriety of . . . teaching *about* religions, as distinguished from the teaching *of* religion, in the public schools," and Justice Clark wrote, "one's education is not complete without a study of comparative religion or the history of religion and its relationship to the advancement of civilization." [3]

Thus the way is legally open, without infringing the Constitution, to rethink the relationship between religion and education and to include education about religion and religions in public school curricula.[4] This way has, in fact, always been

---

elaborate and well-institutionalized civil religion in America." A note on the chapter ends: "Rather than simply denounce what seems in any case inevitable, it seems more responsible to seek within the civil religious tradition for those critical principles which undercut the everpresent danger of national self-idolization."

3. See Philip H. Phenix, "Religion in the Public Schools," in *Religion and the Public Order* (Chicago: University of Chicago Press, 1965).

4. See James V. Panoch and David L. Barr, *Religion Goes to School* (New York: Harper & Row, 1968). The authors are, respectively, Executive Secretary and Associate Executive Secretary of the Religious Instruction Association in Fort Wayne, Ind., the purpose of which is to promote the proper use of the Bible and teaching about religion in schools.

open, but few people would have been prepared to accept it. Since education, like culture, has in the past been so closely tied to one or another form of religion, perhaps a complete divorce was necessary before the possibility of a new relationship could be examined.

In any case, the conviction is growing among educators and others that a "secular" education, in the sense of one that rules out or ignores any transcendental dimensions to human life, is not a truly human one. For one thing:

> How is it possible to study history or social studies, literature, art, music, or even science without reference to the religious persons or movements that have made important contributions? Religion has played such a vital role in civilization that to avoid or omit it, or to fail to deal with it adequately, would represent faulty scholarship and academic folly. No one interested in good education would deny this essentiality. Religion must be studied where it falls logically and naturally into the regular curriculum areas. In some cases, such study might be extended to an entire unit or even to an entire course.[5]

Still more important, perhaps, is the growing realization that "secularism" is itself a form of "religion" in the sense of a basic stance toward reality, and has no more claim to be the only option presented to students than any other. This kind of secularism has held sway for some time in most non-church-related colleges and universities, but some professor and many students are less and less willing to accept it.

In an article entitled "Confessions of a Former Enlightenment Fundamentalist," the sociologist of religion Robert Bellah describes his conversion from a mentality which rigidly adheres to the tenets of the eighteenth-century Enlightenment in much the same way as a religious Fundamentalist holds every book in the Bible to be literal truth:

5. J. Blaine Fister, "Teaching Religion in the Public Schools," *The Living Light*, vol. 6, no. 3 (Fall, 1969), p. 25.

This is the view that science and historical scholarship have effectively disposed of fallacious religious beliefs. If the study of religion has any place in the university at all, which is doubtful to enlightenment fundamentalists, it is to disclose the true reasons why religious believers have been so misguided. The present student generation is not at all prepared to accept these presuppositions. . . .

What I have come to see in the last five years . . . is that I was offering an alternative religious view of my own, but a peculiarly desiccated one, because utterly conceptual, that was designed to cope with the great issues of religion mainly by screening them out in a maze of intellectualization. I don't mean that all my concepts and analyses were wrong. For their limited purposes I think most of them were right. But they were attempting to carry a burden of illicit implication out of all proportion to their usefulness.

In trying to extricate myself from what I now see as an untenable situation I have not attempted to avoid taking a religious position. On the contrary, I have come to see that whatever fundamental stance one takes in teaching about religion is itself a religious position. What I have tried to do is avoid having my own view color everything that gets across in the course and subject my own position to conscious critical analysis.

Specifically, in teaching my course last year I no longer began with an articulated conceptual scheme and then moved toward concrete examples. Rather I began with an attempt to get the students to face the religious dimension of existence directly, to some extent chaotically and without concepts. To this end I included a great deal of religious utterance in my early lectures, often poetry. . . . I used a film of a primitive ritual. . . . I did gradually introduce concepts, trying to indicate how provisional they were, what their uses and limits were, and some of the alternative concepts for dealing with the same problems. . . .

I required a term paper which had to be based on a religious event observed or participated in at first hand. . . . The range of papers was remarkable—from Pentecostal church meetings to LSD trips, from profound experiences of nature to apprehensions of the sacred in group experiences. And best of all they were as rewarding for me to read as they seemed to be the students to write. Several of the students said to me, "I have been waiting years for the chance to write that paper." [6]

A considerable number of psychologists, sociologists, and anthropologists are experiencing the same kind of shift from "enlightenment fundamentalism" to a new openness to the varieties and implications of "man's search for meaning." For example, such authorities as Victor Frankl, Erich Fromm, Abraham Maslow, Carl Rogers, and Erik Erikson maintain, in different ways and with different emphases, that persons become more fully human the more they engage in a search for the deepest meanings of man's existence and for what are truly human values. Although such men are often not themselves believers, they are actively concerned in fostering these values for themselves and others, and view a self-critical faith as a key resource in the unending struggle against idolatry.

Moreover, a very practical concern is the rising wave of interest, at all levels but particularly among young people, in any and every form of "religious" or "transcendental" or "mystical" or occult experience, from Zen Buddhism to witchcraft.[7] Surely they should be provided with some guidelines as to where these various paths have led in the past, some maps of the experiences of the human race in its search for the dimensions of life beyond the observable and the measurable.

In response to these newly felt needs, various approaches are being worked out for courses about religion and religions

6. *Bulletin of the Council on the Study of Religion,* vol. 1, no. 3 (December, 1970).

7. For a highly informative (and disturbing), although not very deep, description of the current scene, see John Charles Cooper, "Religion in the Age of Aquarius (Philadelphia: Westminster Press, 1971).

which would be appropriate and practical for public use, and are being tried out in high schools scattered across the country —one report states that at least 84 schools were involved last year.

One approach is simply to include a study of the religious persons, movements, etc., that have influenced history, literature, social studies, art, and science, in the course of studying these disciplines. This raises no great problem if it could be done merely on a factual level. But, obviously, any real discussion of any book of the Bible as literature, for example, would have to take up its interpretation. The degree of consensus reached in modern scholarship would make this task feasible in terms of what the authors were trying to say. But, if the student is to be helped to seek meanings and values for his own life, he will ask, "What has this got to say *to me?*" Even here, objectivity, though difficult, would still be possible through the exploration of different answers, given by different Judaic and Christian traditions, with no one proposed as *the* answer.[8]

Another approach is the study of religion as a human phenomenon through a comparative study of the great world religions. Here the further possibility exists of inviting committed believers in the different religions studied to make the presentation, and also (where this is feasible) of giving students some experience of the prayers and ceremonies of different religious communities.

A third method, worked out by Philip Phenix of Columbia University, is the study of religion through the various disciplines. His course

> starts with the history, literature, art, and drama of various religions, moving through anthropology, sociology and psychology, as each looks at the phenomenon of religion more scientifically and singularly, and coming full circle to comprehensiveness in

8. See the articles by Phenix and Fister cited in footnotes 3 and 5, above.

a study of religion that touches such diverse thinkers as Anselm, Hegel, Kierkegaard and Thomas Aquinas. Such a course is naturally inappropriate until college level, but modifications following the principles might make such study possible somewhat earlier.[9]

The concerned parent or pastor is probably saying at this point, "But won't such courses lead to young people's thinking that one religion is just as good as another?" Obviously, this could be a real danger if the teacher himself is indifferent to the varying values and emphases of the different religions studied, and a teacher with the "enlightenment fundamentalist" attitude mentioned earlier would be a still greater hazard. But when properly taught by a teacher with the kind of respect and understanding of religion and religions achieved by Robert Bellah, such courses seem rather to help the students not only to grow toward such a respect and understanding themselves, but also to see the need for some positive religious commitment on their own part. After a course in comparative religion given at Arapahoe Senior High School in Littleton, Colorado, for instance, some of the students' comments ran:

Well, I'm learning that not everybody has the same ideas, I mean religious beliefs, that I do, and it's kinda neat finding out how all the religions got started.

I'm learning what religion really means—you know, how it really affects us.

And the parents said:

Educating our kids about the way people believe is great. It's the only way to stop our bigotry and suspicion of each other. Wish we had had courses like it when I was young.

9. Sister Maria Harris, C.S.J., "Four Programs of Religious Study: An Exploration," *The Living Light*, vol. 7, no. 3 (Fall, 1970), pp. 10 ff.

My son's attitude—which is pretty much the same as his friends'—about religion and church has been pretty negative. We were surprised but happy when he decided to take the course.[10]

Or again, I asked a friend in his mid-twenties how he would account for the fact that he is still a practicing Catholic while his brothers, three and five years younger, have discarded the practice of any religion. After some thought, he said, "I guess those courses in different religions I took in college had a lot to do with it. They helped me get things in perspective. Jim and John didn't have anything like that in the colleges they went to."

Moreover, such courses seem to provide one kind of help which a number of young people want from their elders in their search for meaning in life. For example, two studies made at Boston University in 1969 manifested "appreciative evaluations of the Religion Department, and the experience of individual students in specific courses. The . . . scores were the highest for any religiously oriented program, and were coupled with an interest in and need for more course experience." [11] The establishment or expansion of Religious Studies departments in many departments in many colleges and universities would seem to indicate the same desire.

In short, evidence of many kinds shows that numbers of young people today are concerned about the meaning of life and their relationship to the Ultimate, but that they want information about and experience of the answers offered by various religions and philosophies and then to be allowed to work out things for themselves. They are, apparently, not about to accept passively and uncritically the religion they were brought up in,

10. Esther Kronenberger, "Teaching about Religions in a Public School," *The Living Light*, vol. 7, no. 4 (Winter, 1970), pp. 128–129.

11. William A. Overholt, "College Students and Religion in an Urban University," *The Living Light*, vol. 7, no. 3 (Fall, 1970), p. 35.

but they do want the "makings" for an intelligent commitment. Should they not be encouraged and given the best possible in this search, rather than to have their parents' convictions forced on them—an attempt that seems hopeless anyway?

Young people may, indeed, wander far from Christian belief and practice in the course of their search—perhaps to return in time, perhaps not. A friend of ours in her twenties, whose years of Catholic training had left her deeply embittered against the Church, after many experiments has begun again to find meaning in life through Transcendental Meditation which, she says, is not a "religion." Having taken a six-week course in its theory and practice, she now feels that she may soon be able and want to re-examine Christian belief and the experience of God as interpreted and expressed in Christian tradition. While everyone who "leaves the Church" does not arrive at such openness, let alone at a new commitment to Christianity, some do.

For all these reasons, then, it seems that Catholics should join in the efforts of the various educational and religious bodies that are trying to promote courses about religion and religions in public schools and in colleges in whatever way they can.[12] It seems also that we should encourage such courses in Catholic high schools and institutions of higher learning, and in out-of-school programs both for adolescents and for adults.

Parents and others are, very naturally, also deeply concerned lest, in abandoning the "faith of our fathers," young people will abandon also the morality inculcated by that faith. Here again, the most realistic policy would seem to be that of gradu-

12. The most useful tool available for finding out what is being done, what might be done, and why it should be done in this area, together with information about materials and resources, is the boxed kit entitled *Teaching about Religion in the Public Schools*, distributed by the Pennsylvania Council of Churches, obtainable from the Committee on Religion and Public Education, Pennsylvania Council of Churches, 900 South Arlington Ave., Harrisburg, Penna. 17109. It includes reprints of the articles by Phenix and Fister mentioned earlier.

ally helping young people to understand the reasons for moral codes and precepts, that is, the human values which these are meant to protect and foster. Many Christians, unfortunately, still consider the Ten Commandments and the Church's moral teachings to be arbitrary rules imposed by God which mainly forbid us to do enjoyable things. The so-called new morality, although sometimes presented in too glib a fashion, is trying to express Christian teaching in a more positive and helpful way, in the perspective of the two great commandments of love of God and neighbor. Such an approach, obviously, needs to be implemented through a process of positive moral development.

Clearly, any kind of moral education, whether carried out at home or elsewhere, must take into consideration the person's stage of intellectual and emotional maturity. A great deal of research has been done on the stages of moral development which, interestingly enough, corresponds fairly closely to an expression in psychological terms of the age-old biblical notion that "the fear of God is the beginning of wisdom," but that "perfect love drives out fear," and consequently a maturing person should come to act rightly out of love rather than fear. Lawrence Kohlberg, for example, building on Jean Piaget's pioneering efforts, has developed a scheme of the stages of moral development which he has found to apply to young people in our own culture and in Great Britain, Canada, Taiwan, Mexico, and Turkey.

Stage 1: Obedience and punishment orientation. Egocentric deference to superior power or prestige, or a trouble-avoiding set. Objective responsibility.

Stage 2: Instrumental Relativists (IR). Naively egoistic orientation. Right Action is that instrumentally satisfying the self's needs and occasionally others'. Awareness of relativism of value to each actor's needs and perspective. Naive egalitarianism and orientation to exchange and reciprocity.

Stage 3: Personal Concordance (PC). Good-boy orientation. Orientation to approval and to pleasing and helping others.

Conformity to stereotypical images of majority or natural role behavior, and judgment by intentions.

Stage 4: Law and Order (LO). Authority and social-order maintaining orientation. Orientation to "doing duty" and to showing respect for authority and maintaining the given social order for its own sake. Regard for earned expectations of others.

Stage 5: Social Contract (SC). Contractual legalistic orientation. Recognition of an arbitrary element or starting point in rules or expectations for the sake of agreement. Duty defined in terms of contract, general avoidance of violations of the will or rights of others, and majority will and welfare.

Stage 6: Individual Principles (IP). Conscience or principle orientation. Orientation not only to actually ordained social rules but to principles of choice involving appeal to logical universality and consistency. Orientation to conscience as a directing agent and to mutual respect and trust.[13]

Obviously, this scheme need not be taken as the perfect and final description of stages of moral development, but its general validity can be recognized with regard to growing children—and ourselves. And it is useful in suggesting what kinds of motivations for behaving in one way or another might be most persuasive at each stage. For instance, to tell a small child, "Do that to please God" is unrealistic. He hasn't yet achieved the stage of actively wanting to *please* even his parents—let alone the God whom he can't see. If he responds to such a motivation, it will be because he senses that you, the power-figure in his life, intend to make him do it.

This scheme might also be helpful as a general guide to the

13. This statement of Kohlberg's Moral Judgment Scale is taken from Charles Hampden-Turner, *Radical Man*, pp. 120–121, with a reference to "Stage and Sequence: The Cognitive-Developmental Approach to Socialization" by Lawrence Kohlberg, in *Handbook of Socialization Theory and Research*, ed. by David A. Goslin (Chicago: Rand McNally, 1969), p. 376.

kind of explanations of commands and rules made by parents, teachers, and other authorities which would be most understandable to children at different stages of development. "Because I'll spank you" may be the only reason a small child can respond to when you tell him he mustn't cross the street. But he will soon be old enough to understand, "You must look both ways carefully before you cross, because if you don't you might get badly hurt." If parents and teachers thus try to make clear to growing children in ways that they can understand the values to be protected or fostered by their commands, then they will be prepared later to look for and respond to the deeper and higher values expressed in ethical systems and Christian teaching.

But, besides explaining the reasons for their and others' commands and rules, parents and teachers need to entrust children with making whatever decisions they are capable of handling without undue danger to themselves or others, and allow them to learn from their mistakes. A seven-year-old can begin to make his or her own choice of clothes, for instance, in a given price-range, or to decide what he will do with his time among a number of options—as open schools try to do. More complex decisions can be gradually handed over as the children mature, so that they will reach adolescence with some degree of the ability which our tradition calls the virtue of prudence, that is, the habit of making wise decisions. As things are, too frequently young people are suddenly faced with innumerable complex and loaded choices—about drinking, drugs, companions, their future —without any such preparation.

Obviously, the ability to make wise decisions is the component of many abilities—and some of us may not realize how many until we discover, having made some major decision, that we failed to use one or more of them. Our family once bought a house in the middle of winter when its roof was covered with heavy snow, and took the realtor's word that it was in "good condition." When the snow melted we discovered—what anyone on the street could have told us if we had asked—that the roof was badly in need of expensive repairs. We had failed very obviously to apply two of the abilities listed by St. Thomas Aquinas as elements of prudence: to gain all the relevant information and to ask advice. The others he names are: to ascertain the underlying values and issues involved, to make sure that all the factors are taken into account, to reason logically, to proceed step by step, to foresee the consequences of one or another course of action, and to use one's own inventiveness and resourcefulness in arriving at a final decision.

Among these, the ability to recognize the values involved is obviously the most important in the sense that the values one chooses to foster by a decision are, ultimately, what it is all about. In deciding whether to vote for candidate Jones rather than Smith, the first information one wants is about his values, his aims, and then how effectively he can be expected to implement them. Happily, "value clarification" has become what might almost be called a movement today, helping people bring to consciousness—again in ways appropriate to their age and needs—the reasons for their behavior, the values they are trying to protect or foster.

A value, as defined by the authors of the handbook, *Values and Teaching*, must be chosen freely, from among alternatives, after thoughtful consideration of the consequences of each alternative. It must be prized and cherished, publicly affirmed if necessary, and acted on repeatedly.[14] The authors of this handbook developed the various techniques described in it in response to their conviction that many children are apathetic, uncooperative, underachieving, and so on, because they have been exposed to so many different and conflicting values and value systems—from their families, the media, their peers, their

14. Louis E. Raths, Merrill Harmin, Sidney B. Simon, *Values and Teaching: Working with Values in the Classroom* (Columbus, Ohio: Charles E. Merrill Publishing Co., 1966).

schools—and so are confused as to why they should act consistently or bother to act at all.

This is, of course, true to a greater or less extent of all of us, adults as well as children: we act in some areas in virtue of values which we have never examined and which may be in direct conflict with those we believe we profess. Americans profess the value of their country as "the land of the free," for instance, but only recently has it become obvious how many of us are acting, intentionally or not, to prevent its being the land of the free for many minority groups. Christians profess "love of neighbor" as an absolute value, but we are now painfully discovering how unlike Jesus' our judgments have been as to who is our neighbor.

Values and Teaching outlines various techniques to help children sort out their values: the "clarifying response," for instance, opens out a line of thought for the student to take up or not, as he wishes:

> Imagine a student on the way out of class who says, "Miss Jones, I'm going to Washington, D.C., this weekend with my family." How might a teacher respond? Perhaps, "That's nice," or "Have a good time!" Neither or these responses is likely to stimulate clarifying thought on the part of the student. Consider a teacher responding in a different way, for example: "Going to Washington, are you? Are you glad you're going?" To sense the clarifying power in that response, imagine the student saying, "No, come to think of it, I'm not glad I'm going. I'd rather play in the Little League game." If the teacher were to say nothing else at this point other than perhaps, "Well, we'll see you Monday . . ." we might say that the student would be a little more aware of his life; in this case, his doing things he is not happy about doing. This is not a very big step, and it might not be a step at all, but it might contribute to his considering a bit more seriously how much of his life he should involve in things he does not prize or cherish.[15]

15. *Ibid.*, pp. 51–52.

This is obviously a most appropriate and feasible technique for parents to use, as well as teachers, and many of the other methods described in *Values and Teaching*—the "value sheet" which provides a provocative statement and a series of questions, or the "value continuum" on which one marks oneself on a line as more or less for or against some practice or principle— could also be used informally at home (and in so doing might help the parents in their own value clarification). Commercials, movies, and television shows, such as "All in the Family" and those dealing with medical-moral issues, offer other kinds of opportunities for a family to explore and clarify its members' values.[16]

Methods along the lines outlined in *Values and Teaching* are also being used to advantage with adult groups. For example, a minister working with a church group describes the following interesting results of posing in value-continuum form the alternatives: "The American family can best be helped by assisting them to: Develop a prayer life; develop effective family communication."

> All but one of the participants marked far to the side of "Develop a prayer life." The one who marked to the side "Develop effective family communication" was the pastor of the parish. The group was surprised. They remarked how often they had heard that "the family that prays together stays together," and they simply assumed that he would be of that opinion. Likewise, it was soon discovered that since the pastor was present, the group perceived that they should give a "pat" answer. This simple illustration points out the confusion that often exists in the perception of value issues betweeen clergymen and laymen. It points up the untested assumptions people make about one another and their values. These assumptions are often found to be wrong or, at best, misinterpretations.

16. Sidney Simon, "Dinner Table Learning," *Colloquy*, vol. 4, no. 11 (December, 1971), pp. 34 ff., gives some useful suggestions along these lines.

As methods of value clarification for adults, the same author also recommends: a *Beef Box* in which the members of a group can place unsigned "concern cards" (about general life problems) and "complaint cards" (about the group's workings), to be read aloud on occasion and, perhaps, discussed; *voting* by hand-raising on feelings about important personal and social issues; role-playing; reaction forms ("Yes," "No," "Maybe" answers to value statements); and *ranking values* of various kinds in order of importance (e.g., Law and Order, Justice, Freedom).[17]

Obviously, these methods of value clarification do not attempt to impose, inculcate, or "teach" values, but simply to help people disentangle values to which they are enthusiastic about committing themselves in action and word, from the welter of values consciously and unconsciously communicated to them. This whole approach, then, however helpful for this particular purpose, may seem to bypass the question: how can we communicate the values we consider authentically human and humanizing to children or to anyone else?

It seems to me that we can do no more than what has been suggested in this chapter: help children as they are growing up to understand the reasons for our commands and rules, in appropriate terms, and for Christian moral teachings—that is, the values these rules and teachings are designed to protect and foster; help them cultivate the abilities required to make wise decisions; help them clarify their values; and, above all, carry on ourselves the process of *valuing*, that is, of clarifying our own values, prizing and cherishing them, affirming them consistently in word and act, in the light of Christian faith and hope, with the help of the Holy Spirit.

At the end of a very weighty symposium, its organizer, Arthur Koestler, remarked: "Let me close with my favorite motto—a

17. William C. Behrens, "The Confrontation of Values," *The Living Light*, vol. 8, no. 2 (Summer, 1971), p. 65.

sentence I read in a science fiction magazine: 'I have yet to see any problem, however complicated, which, when you looked at it the right way, did not become still more complicated.' " (Poul Anderson).[18]

This motto certainly applies to the problems of religious education and education today, from whatever viewpoint one tries to analyze them. But I hope that these last three chapters have at least served to bring out the fact that a basic educational choice confronts us today. Believing that Christian faith has something unique to contribute to human development, are we nonetheless willing, not to try to *impose* this faith, but rather to *propose* it as desirable? Are we, then, through our attitudes, actions, and words willing to give up trying to mold or form people, young or old, to any predetermined image of what "a good American" and "a good Christian" should be like, and devote ourselves—in the light and strength of this faith—to helping one another, in the Church and in our world, to grow in freedom, honesty, community, and courage?

We cannot help making this choice, by intention or by default, with regard to our own continuing education and to that of those for whom we may responsible, in our particular capacity as members of our Church, of our community, our world. As I hope these three chapters have brought out, the possibilities of making the second choice are at once clearer and greater than ever before in Christian history, because of the peculiar ferment of our times. Can we afford not to take advantage of them?

Peter Berger has recently stated his conviction that the time has come for the Christian community to take "a stance of authority," by which he means "the authority of those who have come to terms with their own experience and who are convinced that, in however imperfect a measure, they have grasped some

18. *Beyond Reductionism*, New Perspectives in the Life Sciences, the Albach Symposium, ed. Arthur Koestler and J. R. Smythus (Boston, Mass.: Beacon Press, 1971), p. 427.

important truths about the human condition." [19] If we keep the above-mentioned possibilities in mind, together with hope in the God in whom we believe, we may be able to face the problems of Catholic schools, of religious education programs, and of what may be promising lines of development for the future, with at least something of such a "stance of authority," of conviction as to what we are about.

19. "A Call for Authority in the Christian Community," *The Christian Century*, Oct. 27, 1971.

6
What about Catholic Schools?

IT IS ESTIMATED THAT, at the present time, Catholic schools are closing on an average of one a day. But, of course, not only Catholic schools are in trouble; all schools are—except in those fortunate areas without acute economic problems, and with an enlightened public and a public school system that can afford to be innovative. Perhaps the present crisis may force the kind of rethinking of the role of schools as such in our society suggested in earlier chapters, and with it a rethinking of methods of funding which will make it possible for our society to provide adequate and varied educational opportunities for everyone.

In the meantime, we Catholics have a special responsibility to try to solve our own school problems in such a way as not to add to the problems of the public schools but, rather, to do whatever can be done in different circumstances to improve educational conditions. The purpose of this chapter, then, is to consider various possibilities of making creative use of the present very difficult situation in such a way as to help rather than harm our society and our Church. What kind of schools should we try to maintain or establish? How might we dispose of the others so as to benefit rather than harm education in a given area?

Catholic schools have, of course, until fairly recently been almost universally considered *the* great educational asset of the American Catholic Church, just as schools in general have been made into the central means of education in our society. In line with the questions and suggestions about schools and schooling made in earlier chapters, it would seem that we now need to ask about any given Catholic school or school system: is it, or is it capable of becoming, a subsidiary element in the total educational effort of the parish or area or diocese, rather than its center in the sense of a sponge absorbing all the available attention and interest. Fr. Michael O'Neill [1] is quoted as citing instances of Catholic parishes "where the school closed and suddenly there was a huge hush, silence and vacuum, and it became painfully clear that not much else of interest was going on in the parish."

In many places, Catholic schools have certainly had the effect of excluding other educational efforts, both in the narrower and wider sense: financing and conducting a school is necessarily a very demanding enterprise. But one can imagine situations in which it might be possible to transform a given school into a radiating, out-reaching center, fostering many-sided educational activities for the whole community. Such a school might indeed be an asset to the Church, whereas the sponge type surely is not. But such a transformation of the school would require a previ-

---

1. In National Catholic Reporter, October 29, 1971. The heading of the article, also a quote from Fr. O'Neill, is "Aid Isn't School Answer." He is the author of *New Schools in a New Church* (St. John's University Press, Collegeville, Minn. 1971, paper).

ous transformation of its constituency's notions of what a "school" should do.

Again, in view of the choice posed at the end of the previous chapter, the question also needs to be asked: what kind of Catholic school is truly an asset to the Church today and is this given school capable of becoming what is needed? Will Catholics support it if it is trying to provide a truly human and humanizing education, opening out Christian faith as a worthwhile option but not trying to impose it? We shall have to return to this problem again, since it is bound up with all the questions we have been considering in the course of this book.

In seeking public funding for Catholic schools, a great deal of effort is now being spent on trying to convince the public that Catholic schools are not only an asset to the Church but a very valuable asset to our nation. Certainly, if Catholic schools are to exist at all, they should be a national "asset" as part of the Church's service of human well-being. But, here again, questions need to be asked: if the given school or system tends to promote racial or economic segregation, or to downgrade the quality of public education, is it truly an asset to the community or the nation? Obviously no generalizations should be made for the country as a whole, and there will surely be areas in which hard-pressed and already overcrowded public school administrators will be grateful that Catholic schools can continue to service a significant percentage of the population. But this is not always the case. I visited a middle-sized town recently which had had no Catholic schools before 1960, when its public schools were generally considered excellent. Since then, it has acquired two parochial grade schools, one parochial girls' high school and a diocesan boys' high school. Four or five quite different people told me that since these schools were established the quality of public education has steadily declined. Thus a vicious circle has been set up: as the public schools deteriorate, fewer and fewer parents concerned about quality education want to send their children to them, and the schools continue to deteriorate and to be populated more and more exclusively by underprivileged children—a vicious circle all too evident on a much larger scale in many big cities. Have these Catholic schools, then, truly been an asset to their community?

Again, is a Catholic school or school system a national asset, or rather a liability, if it mainly provides the noneducational functions mentioned earlier: custodial care, ladder-and-labeling, and domestication for a considerable number of children, thus saving the public the responsibility of providing for them?

This is, of course, in large part the same question raised earlier in connection with a school's value to the Church. In trying to answer both questions, imaginative and creative Catholic school people are dreaming of, and trying to work toward, schools which would be truly liberating "communities of love." Free of the bureaucracy and political stresses that afflict so many public school systems, they would be at liberty to try out the most promising educational theories and practices. They would offer a real alternative to public education and provide a stimulus to the public schools to compete with them in excellence. As was suggested above, they might, further, become centers of community education, involving parents and members of the community actively in many capacities, and so giving them opportunities to educate one another.[2]

This is an inspiring ideal, and many Catholic educators and schools are working toward it in different ways. Almost every issue of *Momentum*, a publication of the National Catholic Educational Association, carries some reports of innovative schools and programs along one or more of the lines suggested in Chapter 4. In ghetto areas particularly, some Catholic schools

2. See, for example, C. Albert Koob and Russell Shaw, *S.O.S. for Catholic Schools* (Holt, Rinehart and Winston, 1971), Ch. 7, and the interview with Fr. Koob, who is president of the National Catholic Educational Association, headed, "From the parochial school to 'total education' programs," in *National Catholic Reporter*, October 16, 1970.

are trying to provide a truly liberating education. De Porres High School in Detroit, for example, has as its purpose:

> To help the students determine a basis of values for making decisions and judgments; to develop a sense of dignity and worth of self as a person and, consequently, of the worth of all persons. The values that we have decided to stress are those of self-worth, confidence in personal abilities, respect for others and sensitivity to the world and its people. What we are talking about are universal human and, of course, Christian values, but we want our students to find a black style of incarnating and fostering them. To achieve this purpose two separate departments were created to replace the existing Religion Department: a Department of Human Relations offering courses in sociology, psychology and philosophy, and a Department of Catechetics which would deal directly with the faith of Christian believers. The catechetics department will not be academically oriented nor will it be obligatory for any student to attend. This factor of freedom will give a serious tone that has been missing in many approaches to a religious education program. When a student comes to a catechetics meeting, he will want to come, and will know why he is coming and what will be discussed.[3]

But to implement this ideal on anything like a large scale raises various problems. For one thing, to be or to become this kind of school would require funding which would leave the school free to formulate and carry out its own educational policies. Perhaps methods of funding private schools with public money can be worked out which would allow such freedom. But the Catholic schools in Rhode Island, for instance, to whom state aid was refused by the recent Supreme Court decisions, had agreed that their teachers who were to receive salary supplements from public funds would teach "only those subjects required to be taught

3. Raymond Mack, "A Value-Centered Religious Education for an Inner City High School," *The Living Light*, vol. 6, no. 4, Winter, 1969.

by state law or which are provided in public schools throughout the state, or any other subjects that are taught in the public schools" and use only materials used in the schools of the state (R.I.Gen. Laws Ann. #16–51). If such conformity is the price of continued existence, is it worth while continuing to exist? Do not Catholic schools have the responsibility of contributing to educational improvement precisely by offering substantially *different* kinds of education from that provided in the public schools?

The voucher plan proposed in *A Report on Financing Elementary Education by Grants to Parents,* prepared by the Center for the Study of Public Policy [4] under a grant from the U.S. Office of Economic Opportunity, does not require such conformity. On the contrary, its objective is precisely to provide a variety of educational options to poor parents as well as to the more affluent, and to give parents, and particularly disadvantaged parents, more control over the kind of education their children get. This voucher plan, indeed, with its carefully worked-out safeguards against segregation, commercialism, and many other undesirable results foreseen from other such plans, seems to be an economic design likely to further the objectives toward which Catholics should be working in education. In some areas, where a diversified and flexible public school system exists, serving the needs of all socio-economic groups, the ques-

4. This Report by the Center for Public Policy (56 Boylston St., Cambridge, Mass. 02138) is well worth studying, with its thorough analysis of the economic workings of the present "system" and proposed alternatives. Particularly provocative, perhaps, is the suggestion that the traditional definitions of "public" and "private" schools classify schools in terms of *who* runs them, not *how* they are run. If we want to understand what is really going on in education, we might well reverse this emphasis. We would then call a school "public" if it were open to everyone on a nondiscriminatory basis, if it charged no tuition, and if it provided full information about itself to anyone interested. Conversely, we would call any school "private" if it excluded applicants in a discriminatory way, charged tuition, or withheld information about itself (pp. 13–14).

tion would certainly need to be asked whether adoption of this voucher plan would tend to weaken something already fairly good without substantially improving the situation. But so many public school systems, especially in large cities, appear so hopeless that providing alternatives seems the only possible method of providing better education for more children. Moreover, this plan might make possible far more rapid changes for the better in our total educational "system" than would otherwise occur, by making it possible for innovative schools and programs to survive.

At the time of writing, no voucher experiments are actually in operation. OEO is still in active negotiation with several districts, however, and several are receiving funds from OEO for feasibility studies. Nobody knows whether the participation of church-related schools in such a plan would be considered constitutional, but the Report gives some impressive arguments as to why it might be. New, to the writer at least, is the theory "that the essential feature of the voucher program—its reliance on individual freedom of choice—makes it constitutionally immune. The premise of this theory is that the voucher program puts effective control of the educational funds in private hands. Since private acts which benefit religion are constitutionally protected, it is arguable that a voucher program is constitutionally protected even if benefits accrue to the religious school receiving the vouchers." Cited in this connection is the case of Quick Bear v. Luepp (210. U.S. 50. L905), concerning the cost of salaries and maintenance of a Catholic school on an Indian reservation. The Indians were entitled to the funds for a school by a treaty and, consequently, "the government had no choice but to allocate them once the Indians determined their disposition by choosing the schools they wished to attend." The Supreme Court upheld the expenditures, noting that the funds were, in effect, not spent by the Federal Government but administered by it. "Thus *Quick Bear* indicates that aid to a religious school may be held constitutional if two conditions are met: entitlement to the money, and private choice as to its ultimate recipient. Each of these requirements is met in a voucher program." [5]

This theory has the great advantage of making it unnecessary to try to distinguish between the "secular" and "religious" aspects of the education a particular school provides—a distinction which, as we saw in an earlier chapter, is increasingly being recognized as an unreal one, although it provided the main basis for the Supreme Court's decision in the DiCenso and Lemon cases.

To promote the Report's voucher plan would, therefore, seem much worthier of Catholics' long-range efforts than the tax credit plan currently proposed by the bishops of the United States as the most feasible solution to Catholic schools' financial problems. The basic ingredient of this latter is a provision that would allow parents to be reimbursed by the government for up to one half of the money they spent on tuition and fees, the reimbursement to come in the form of a federal income tax credit. As Bishop McManus admitted, this plan "gives no break" to parents who are so poor that they don't have to pay taxes.[6]

Moreover, as the OEO Report remarks, tax credit plans, like most of the bills and acts other than the voucher system designed to assist non-public schools, "are designed to save the taxpayer money. None provides enough money to finance new or innovative schools. They are also designed to preserve the existing range of public and parochial alternatives, not to broaden it." [7] But broadening this range should be precisely one of the aims of maintaining or establishing a Catholic school.

5. *Ibid.*, pp. 222–224.

6. Quoted in *National Catholic Reporter*, Dec. 10, 1971. Bishop McManus added that through the Campaign of Human Development the Church is working to help people make enough money to pay taxes, and that the bishops are continuing to promote the Elementary and Secondary Education Act, the heart of which, Title I, provides special services for socio-economic disadvantaged children.

7. *Op. cit.*, p. 90.

We may hope, then, whether or not this tax credit plan succeeds as an immediate measure for giving Catholic schools a breathing-space, as it were, in which to plan their future, that long-range efforts would be directed toward promoting the OEO Report's voucher plan in the areas where this would be likely to benefit all children's education.

The constitutionality of "shared time" or "dual enrollment" has, at the time of writing, still to be tested in the Supreme Court. In this plan, Catholic students attend classes in so-called value-free subjects in the public schools, or lease classrooms for these subjects to the public schools, and the classes are taught by teachers paid by the public schools.

This is one way of getting public money for what are, by and large, the most expensive areas of modern education: the sciences, physical education, and "shop." It is also a way of avoiding the harm to a public school system and the burden on the taxpayers which would be caused by the complete closing of Catholic schools: the system has to take over only certain areas of the Catholic children's education.

But do Catholics wish to encourage educational structures that perpetuate the schizophrenic division between the sciences (which, as too many students are convinced, teach what is "true") and the humanities (which teach merely opinion)? At a time when leading scientists are themselves beginning to realize the relativity of their constructs of reality and the relative validity of other ways of approaching it—through the arts, through philosophy, through religion—do we want to encourage by dual enrollment a view of the "really real" as only what is quantifiable and measurable and what everybody can agree upon, a view which has helped to bring us to our present plight? Do we want to encourage the essentially irreligious and anti-human notion that there are "value-free" subjects or areas of human knowledge and behavior?

Dual enrollment, then, may well be the only immediate alternative to working a greater injustice on public education and taxpayers by suddenly closing Catholic schools. But whether or not it should be considered as anything more than a temporary solution, even if it is certified as a constitutional one, is a question that needs very careful thinking out.

In *Can Catholic Schools Survive?* William E. Brown argues with an impressive array of figures that Catholics and other religious groups could support their own schools through tax-deductible contributions to their churches, and even persuade businesses to help them, and that this would cost them less than the extra taxes that would have to be levied to provide public school education for the same numbers of children.

> The more children who are educated in private schools, the less extra cost it is to each of the groups that maintain those schools, because fewer children are in the public schools and taxes are less. Obviously, too, extra cost will be minimized (and may turn into a saving) if per pupil cost is kept lower than in the public schools and *contributions* are the means of financing.[8]

I have not seen a serious critique of Brown's proposal from the financial point of view, and have no competence to offer one. But let us suppose that it is feasible. The question would then, once more, be whether Catholics generally are prepared to support schools which are truly assets to the Church and to the nation, how many of them, and where? Such schools would, obviously, not be for an elite only or for Catholics only; they would have to be open to any children whose parents wanted them to have the particular kind of educational experience

8. William E. Brown and Andrew M. Greeley, *Can Catholic Schools Survive?* (Sheed & Ward, N.Y., 1970). Also William E. Brown's pamphlet, *The Response Ability To Supply the Financial Requirements of a Roman Catholic Diocese and Its Parishes* (Obtainable from the author, 920 E. Mason St., Milwaukee, Wisc., 53202). The quotation is from the pamphlet, p. 13.

which the school was offering.[9] These schools could not be used as a means to any kind of racial or class segregation. Nor would they attempt to indoctrinate young people or "form" students to be committed Catholics; they would follow the lines of the De Porres statement of purpose quoted above. It seems to me, then, that as things are, while a diocese might be prepared to support a few such schools—and many dioceses do—the Catholic public generally would need to clarify and change its views as to the purpose of Catholic schools before it would support them on a large scale.[10]

But even if it were ready to do so, or if the financial problems

9. This openness is laid down as a requirement in the Statement of the Bishops of the Boston Province on Catholic Schools, issued in November, 1971: "The schools we retain must be good schools, sensitive to the needs of young people in today's world, models of what a true Christian community can accomplish even in the midst of a world preoccupied with selfish and materialistic concerns. The goals we seek here are lofty and difficult; with good will and the spirit of Christian love, they can be reached. In addition, we must always remember that our schools must serve all, the rich, the poor, and the average citizen. We must take it as our goal to see to it that their doors are open, insofar as possible, to all. This specific responsibility is a burden which must be assumed by the total Christian community."

10. *Directions for the Future for Catholic Schools in the Archdiocese of Chicago*, a report of its School Study Commission, August, 1971, looks toward a transfer of power and responsibility to local (parish and area) school boards, to plan and implement the kind of education each desires, with the advice and aid of the central Archdiocesan authority. It also "recommends that the 2,500,000 Catholics of the Archdiocese of Chicago and their parishes give high priority to: Catholic schools serving neighborhoods with large numbers of low-income families, such as those in public housing; Catholic schools whose students are predominantly children of newly-arrived immigrants or recent arrivals to the Archdiocese from the South, from Puerto Rico or from Indian reservations. . . . Catholic schools or institutions developing programs for students with special needs (and with a desire for a Catholic education): the deaf, the emotionally disturbed, the over-aged, dropouts, unwed, pregnant teen-age girls, and others with severe needs." One can certainly hope that this recommendation is heeded.

of Catholic schools were to be solved by outside help which left them free, judgments would still have to be made as to whether, in the given situation, the existence of such private schools would strengthen or weaken the whole educational effort in the particular area, as was mentioned earlier in this chapter.

Judgments would also need to be made as to the advantages and disadvantages of conducting such schools under church auspices. If the aim is to improve education in the area, the Catholics concerned might well be more effective if they joined with people who shared their ideas as to a humanizing and liberating education, to start a school under nonsectarian auspices. Here, as in a Catholic school, they could still give their witness to the worthwhileness of Christianity by their style of living and teaching—as many are now doing in both public and private schools. But one can also imagine situations in which it might be a definite advantage for creative and innovative schools to be operated under church auspices, at least to begin with, when this would give them more credibility and solidity.

The criteria, then, for long-range planning to keep a Catholic school in existence or to establish a new one would seem to be these: Can it work toward becoming a true "community of love," providing a truly liberating education? Does it render a service which no other educational agency is providing in a given area or might provide if it did not? Does rendering this service help the total educational effort both of the human and the Christian community in the area?

In the meantime, Catholic schools are too frequently closing in a haphazard fashion, which harms rather than in any way helps either of these interrelated efforts. Too often, pastors and people feel that if they can't have Catholic schools, there is no use making any real efforts to provide religious education: the "save our schools to save souls" mentality is still with us and, where it exists, could become a self-fulfilling prophecy. An article in the *National Catholic Reporter* (Oct. 29, 1971), with the rather dramatic title "From the Ashes Rises a New Hope," describes what has been happening since the Catholic schools in Pueblo, Colorado, were closed, as of the fall of 1971—a closing announced the previous March.

> Now that the schools are closed, said the diocesan business manager, many parishes are in a position to resume making their debt payments and are catching up on maintenance work on parish plants. "But," he added, "they're just coming to the surface in some parishes and it will take time before they can actually put adequate financing into new educational programs!" . . . The prevalent reaction of Pueblo's Catholic community to the new alternate education programs appears to be an attitude of resignation to the fact that the closings were inevitable and a hopeful expectation that the new programs will be able to fill the educational gap.

But the same paper reports in its issue for February 25, 1972, under the heading, "Pueblo CCD Program May Die from Apathy," a "statement of concern," made to Bishop Buswell and released to the press, by the members of the Pueblo Catholic Education Office, saying that:

> People in the diocese, and more specifically in the city of Pueblo, are apathetic toward Catholic education as a result of apathy, bewilderment, confusion, despair and general ignorance (of diocesan programs) on the part of pastors. We see this apathy as a vital problem in our attempt to plan and implement educational programs through the Office of Catholic Education.

Similar frustrations are all too common, both on parish and diocesan levels. At the same time, as we shall see shortly, there are also some signs of hope that a wider and deeper view of Catholic education is beginning to replace, in some quarters at least, the conviction that Catholic schools are a necessity if the Church is to survive. In the developing view, as was noted earlier, many elements of such an education can be provided by other than Catholic agencies. Consequently, will not Catholics be at once benefiting themselves and serving their society by cooperating with "all men of good will" in improving education for everyone, rather than struggling to keep as many Catholic schools, in existence as possible.

In any case, here and now, planning is needed that will provide for the closing of the Catholic schools which are to be closed, for whatever reason, in such a way as to benefit rather than harm the educational effort of the human community in which these schools have been operating.

Some situations might suggest the solution adopted, for example, by what is now the Urban Day School in Milwaukee. This was originally a parochial school which had to be closed for financial reasons. Through the efforts of two of the Sisters who had been teaching in it, it was reopened as a desegregated experimental school, mainly for disadvantaged children, under the auspices of a nonsectarian board, financed by contributions and some foundation grants.

In other situations, the most creative solution might be to lease or to sell the buildings and equipment to the public school system, and encourage the dedicated and qualified teachers and administrators in the Catholic school(s) to try to find work within the public school system and influence it toward a "liberating" education from within. I suggested this possibility to the people in the town mentioned earlier in this chapter, who had been telling me about the deterioration of the public schools since the advent of the Catholic ones, and their eyes lit up: "Wouldn't it be great," they said, "if they could all get together and make the schools in this town really good!" I heard of this actually happening in one small town with a mediocre public high school and a mediocre Catholic one. They merged their resources and the result was one good school. Undoubtedly, similar arrangements have been arrived at elsewhere.

In some situations, might it not even be possible—as it would certainly be an act of Christian witness—to *give* the buildings and equipment to the public school system, perhaps under the condition that they be used for a certain kind of experimental education or to meet some special need?

Still another possibility would be to transform the school buildings into a religious education center, perhaps an ecumenical one, or into a community education center which could include many kinds and levels of religious education in both the broad and the narrow sense of the term.

Undoubtedly, other possibilities will emerge as conditions change and new situations arise. These mentioned are only the most obvious at the moment. But the importance of planning for one or another creative solution *before* closing a school can hardly be overemphasized. It is not the fault of the general public today that its school systems developed without having to provide for the millions of children in Catholic schools. It is not its fault that so many Catholic schools are now in trouble. Nor, indeed, is it the fault of the present generation of Catholics. But it is our responsibility to solve the resulting problems in ways that will aid and not hinder the transformation of our present educational system into a more human and liberating one.

The responsibility for the future of Catholic schools is, increasingly, being shared by, or transferred to, local elected lay boards, rather than being the exclusive prerogative of the pastor and bishop or even the priests' senate ("Directions for the Future for Catholic Schools in the Archdiocese of Chicago" is being proposed as a model). Every Catholic, therefore, needs to become familiar with the total local situation and the possibilities it offers, and to do what he can to see that a creative solution is arrived at. It is, of course, difficult for many, if not most, Catholics to believe that they really do possess any real decision-making power about schools or any other church matters—and, in many places, this power is still merely an advisory one and in others exists only on paper. But it is surely our responsibility to use whatever power we have or might gain with regard to these matters for the good of the total community and the Church, as far as we can discern it.

At the same time, it is our responsibility to find ways of helping one another "grow up in all things toward Christ" as members of smaller or larger Christian communities—families, groups, parishes, dioceses—so that we can make our unique Christian contribution to human liberation and development. In the past, the Catholic school was considered the chief means of such growth, but even the most ardent proponents of the continued usefulness of Catholic schools now realize that they can only be one means among many, that "religious education" must be carried out by many other agencies, in many other ways.

The past few years have seen, in many places at least, an astonishing development in the personnel and resources devoted to religious education programs. One large Archdiocese Office had no budget in 1965 for this purpose; for 1971–72 it is in the vicinity of $96,000, and expects a considerable further increase for the following year. Another reports that its allotment for 1968 was around $30,000, and for 1971 was $270,000. The Office of Religious Education in a smaller diocese, with the responsibility for both school and non-school religious education, reports a present budget of $180,000, covering twelve full-time staff people, specialized in areas and levels, with a $30,000 budget for a Research Center alone. A parish CCD in the midwest had no budget in 1967 but its allotment for 1972 is $41,510.

One might think—and many people do—that these amazing increases are related in direct proportion to the closing of schools. But all those concerned whom I consulted said explicitly that no such correlation exists. In the second diocese mentioned, in fact, only one small school has been closed. They all insist that this increase in resources and personnel is the result of a real upsurge of concern about the religious education of all the Catholic people. As one Diocesan Director put it in a letter:

> It seems strange to me that any increase in CCD budgets or personnel is interpreted by pastors, moderators, religious

communities, the laity and everybody else to mean that schools are closing. Few seem to realize that, no matter what his stand on schools is, the general religious education of our people is a chief priority.

The two following chapters, then, will discuss this "chief priority"—first, in terms of some of the main problems that have arisen, due to this sudden expansion of the field as well as to many other factors and, second, what seem to be the most promising lines for future development.

7
What's Going On
in "Religious Education"?

"WHAT'S GOING ON in religious education?" is a question which few Catholics, until very recently, would have dreamed of asking. Nothing was expected to "go on" in the sense of change or trouble. But today the "field" of religious education is an area—one might almost say, an arena—in which all the problems of the churches and society, of religion and education, converge, collide, interweave. "What's going on?" is a question innumerable people are asking, though in different tones: some expectantly, some hopefully, some anxiously, some desparingly.

At any rate, we do not have to worry for the moment about a decline of interest—as, it seems, some of our Protestant colleagues do. (At a meeting I attended, this decline was proposed as the first topic for discussion. The other Catholic present, a diocesan CCD director, and I looked at each other and ex-

claimed together, "At least that's not one of our problems.")
The growth in diocesan and parish budgets for religious education was mentioned in the previous chapter. In addition might
be cited the fact that some eight thousand people attended a
New England Congress of Religious Education in August 1971
and an equal number a national one in October of the same
year. Or, again, in 1964 there were only some fifty candidates
studying for masters' and twenty-five for doctoral degrees in
religious education, whereas in 1971-2 there are estimated to be
approximately 1850—a figure which includes only those studying
in the thirty-seven Catholic colleges and universities offering
graduate work in this field; there are also many Catholic candidates studying in Protestant institutions. Seven years ago, a
reasonably complete listing of summer courses, workshops, semi-
nars, etc., concerned with religious education could be made on
two pages or so; today such a listing requires the equivalent of a
booklet.

The men and women who attend such programs are, in one
way or another and more or less deeply, affected by the developing ideas in theology and pedagogy discussed earlier in this
book. But when religious educators try to apply them in parishes
and dioceses, the pastors and parents and other Catholics back
home who have not been exposed to these "new notions" often
become concerned about religious education from a completely
different perspective—of bewilderment or downright hostility
to what seem like "radical" ideas.[1]

Conditions vary so greatly from parish to parish, area to area,
diocese to diocese, that anyone who travels around and tries to

1. It seems that "progressive" Jewish and Protestant religious educators
face much the same kinds of discontent, for at least analogous reasons. In
particular, the complaint, "What's this got to do with religious education?" is registered in communications about articles and programs both
in the excellent publication, *Alternatives in Religious Education*, edited by
Audrey Friedman, Director of Education at Temple Micah in Denver,
Colorado, and to *Colloquy*, published by the United Church Board for
Homeland Ministries, Philadelphia, Penna.

assess situations tends to feel more or less hopeful or despairing according to whom he has last spoken with. Any general statements are dangerous to make; they will probably be contradicted by what is happening in the next place visited. However, some problems seem general enough to warrant some discussion as to their causes and possible solutions.

Rapidity of Change

One reason for friction is, obviously, that the various developments we have been discussing have been taking place so rapidly that large numbers of people have not begun to catch up with one before another appeared. As a result, Catholics in many places feel quite strongly that they and their children have been subjected to a haphazard succession of approaches and programs, texts and "aids," in their parish worship and in CCD classes, that they have been experimented with by people who can't make up their minds what they are trying to do or how to do it. And many of the religion teachers who have valiantly tried to understand and use each new approach, method, or "aid" suggested to, or imposed on them, may well feel the same way, only more so.

Of course, if things are to improve, people with competence and imagination must be left reasonably free to try out new ways, to make some mistakes, to try again. How such experimentation could be made a less traumatic experience for all concerned is a question we shall try to deal with both in this chapter and the next.

On the other hand, it is also true that to grow into what we have been calling the developing view of Christian faith and religious education cannot be done overnight. Neither can it be done by taking courses or attending a workshop and then, without time to digest what one has learned and to put it in perspective, come home and start applying it. To grow into this view must be a slow, freely undertaken, and continuing process of coming to look at life in a new perspective and working out the implications of this shift.

Thus it can happen that a well-meaning person, qualified by possessing a degree in "Religious ed." can raise havoc in a parish because he or she has only grasped one partial aspect of the developing view—say, the Christian's vocation to work for social justice. In the desire to emphasize such work as essential to authentic Christianity, he or she may downgrade parishioners' devotions, or their desire to have their children grow familiar with their Christian heritage, thereby antagonizing them while accomplishing nothing. Or it can happen that a part-time teacher who has gone to the workshops set up by the publishers of the text she is to use and become reasonably happy with the "kerygmatic" approach, is thoroughly confused when a new "experiential" series is adopted and she is now told to learn to become a quite different kind of teacher using films and records and "happenings."

Here the publishers of texts and producers of materials tend to play an ambiguous role. They are, in the main, conscientiously trying to implement new approaches of whose value they are convinced. They have and do render great service in setting up workshops, designing teacher-training kits, guides, and the like. But the "experts" on whom they call to produce their materials may not have a balanced view of the new approach they want to implement. At the same time, the loud cries of administrators and teachers for usable materials indicate a market—and publishers and producers of materials are looking for saleable products and want to sell them. They can hardly avoid the Madison Avenue kind of sales-pitch: "This is the newest and best, and just what you need." Administrators and teachers, bewildered themselves, often find it difficult to distinguish between what they really need and can use properly, and what they are told that they need.

One unfortunate result is that many teachers tend to take the latest teaching-aid as *the* solution to their problems. Using films is one current example. A perceptive observer, whose job as a diocesan CCD librarian includes making films available and setting up previews, says that too many CCD teachers in her area seem to select for high school classes films which are far too sophisticated for the teachers themselves to appreciate, in the hope that the students who "understand that sort of thing" will "get the message." [2]

One fairly obvious way out of the problems more or less directly caused by the rapidity of change would be to allow time for the people working in religious education programs in a given parish or area to think out together what they are really trying to accomplish, to deepen their understanding of it, and to consider what kinds of further training and resources will best help them. (They might even discover that they didn't need any texts at all.) Then, when they felt ready, they would propose their plans and the rationale behind them to the parish council, and their plans for children's and young people's programs to parents' and young people's groups. And they would make both presentations, not in the "this is the way it's going to be" style, but rather, "What do you think of this, and how could you help us improve our plans so as to meet your needs better."

As things too often are, a religious education team has to try to find time for such digesting and planning over a holiday weekend or at some other time, in addition to running already-existing programs. The idea of discontinuing *all* programs for half a year or a year, especially programs for children while paying a staff for planning, is one which many pastors and parents find hard to take. But perhaps ways can be found to make it acceptable if it could be shown that such a "retreat" would ulti-

2. See Janet M. Bennett, "You Name It: A Diocesan CCD Librarian's Expanding Job," *The Living Light*, vol. 8, no. 2 (Summer, 1971), p. 133 ff.

mately benefit everyone concerned; we will try to suggest in the next chapter the kind of framework in which this might more generally be possible.

Authoritarianism

Another effect of so many rapid changes is that people who are trying to implement the developing approach find it difficult to rid themselves of some of the attitudes characteristic of the one they were brought up in. They can be just as authoritarian about the "liberating" approach as they were about the "this is what the Church teaches" method. For example, at a meeting to plan a film strip to help parents understand "new ways" of teaching religion, one of the group asked the priest in charge of the project what he thought its main thrust should be. "That they should trust us because we are the experts" was his answer.

The same authoritarianism is very obviously displayed in the way in which parents have been disregarded in introducing new approaches. Texts are now including parents' booklets, and meetings with parents to discuss religious education programs are becoming more and more widespread. It is, surely, more than time. However we define it, the parents' role is primary. For religious educators to disregard the parents, then, is hardly consonant with respect for colleagues in a common task.

Equally authoritarian, and so inconsistent with the developing view are attempts to "get at" parents through their children in ways calculated to increase the generation gap rather than bridging it. It seems to me quite legitimate, for instance, to ask high school students to discuss, "What would you do if you were the Pope?" knowing that some of them will want to continue the discussion at home and hoping that some knowledge will finally be gained by some parents as well as the students about the Pope's authority, the nature of different kinds of church laws, etc.[3] But the kind of "parent education" advocated in the following quotation seems to indicate a very onesided and unwise kind of zeal tending to frustrate its own aims:

> . . . You need the religion course to get to parents and I don't mean just by way of the students, though kids of 16 and 17 are teaching lots of things to lots of parents these days. You reach the parents through the religion program by creating enough questions about the war, poverty, race, and all the other neat things we live with so that the parents come to you hot and bothered with the question, "What's this got to do with religion?" This goodly hassling is happening nationwide now and is probably the only meaningful form of adult education going on in our country.[4]

Many people still do indeed need to have their attention drawn to the massive problems of our society (although, I would think, most of us need still more to be helped to discover what we can effectively do about any of them). But is this a human or humanizing way of doing so—to use young people as a kind of club against their parents?

To talk about "involving parents" in their children's religious education also seems to me to smack of the old authoritarianism. The term itself is essentially meaningless. Parents cannot help being involved, whether they realize it or not, since it is their attitudes and behavior toward each other, their children, other people and life, which first and most strongly influence the children's attitudes and behavior, and thus constitute their basic religious education. This is why parents are inevitably the "primary religious educators" of their children. But they are hardly

3. See Dolores Curran, "The Family that Thinks Together," in *There's More than One Way to Teach Religion,* ed. by Mary Perkins Ryan and Russell J. Neighbor (New York: Paulist Press, 1970).

4. Thomas S. Klise, correspondence, *Commonweal,* Feb. 12, 1971, p. 479.

going to be convinced that they *are* the primary educators by being told that they should be "involved." (See above, chapter 2, for some further suggestions on parents sharing in their children's religious education.)

Of course, the idea of "involving parents," especially in preparation of their children for first Confession and Communion, began to spread at a time when it was assumed that this preparation must include communicating the doctrinal information contained in the No. 1 Baltimore Catechism or the equivalent. (This, by the way, in spite of the fact that the decree of St. Pius X on early Communion lays down only the requirement that the child be able to distinguish the Eucharistic bread from the ordinary bread.) No wonder many parents were alarmed, feeling themselves equipped to be neither theologians nor teachers.

One way of reassuring them has been to offer them classes, both in the "content" and in how to get it across to children, and to provide texts and materials. The effort, in other words, was toward transferring a classroom situation to the home and substituting mother or father (usually mother) for the teacher. Many parents, put in this position, have been feeling more or less resentful that, as one critic put it, at a time when they feel more insecure than ever before, the burden of their children's religious instruction should be imposed on them.

Potentially far more promising efforts to open out to parents the scope of their vocation as Christians and Christian parents— rather than, or in addition to, "involving" them in some particular program—have been spreading recently, again in connection with the children's reception of the sacraments. Parents are urged or, in some places, required to attend a meeting or meetings with the pastor, in groups or privately, before their children may be baptized or receive their first Communion or go to Confession.

This trend has received a certain endorsement from Rome,

in the Introduction to the revised Rite for the Baptism of children which states:

> After baptism it is the responsibility of the parents, in their gratitude to God and in fidelity to the duty they have undertaken, to enable the child to know God, whose adopted child it has become, to receive confirmation, and to participate in the holy Eucharist. In this duty they are to be helped by the parish priest by suitable means. (II, 5).

> It is the duty of the priest to prepare families for the baptism of their children and to help them in the task of Christian formation which they have undertaken. It is the duty of the bishop to coordinate such pastoral efforts in the diocese, with the help also of deacons and lay people. (II, 7, 5).

> When the parents are not yet prepared to profess the faith or to undertake the duty of bringing up their children as Christians, it is for the parish priest, keeping in mind whatever regulations may have been laid down by the conference of bishops, to determine the time for the baptism of infants (III, 8, 4).

The Church has, indeed, in theory at least, always required some assurance that children would be "brought up as Catholics" before allowing them to be baptized. But in practice this has mainly meant an assurance that the children would not be brought up in some other religion or a form of Protestantism; Catholic parents have not been required to give evidence of the reality of their profession of the faith or of their determination to bring up their children as Christians.

I have discussed this question with several pastors who make some form of parental commitment and/or instruction a requirement for children's baptism. They say that because of it they have reached people to whom their children's baptism would have otherwise been a mere formality, and that if such people had only been invited and not required to meet with the pastor, they would not have come. They say further that a large number of Catholics are used to being treated like children and ordered to do this or that by church authorities, and that laying down such requirements is the only way to reach them to help them mature as Christians. Still further, they say very reasonably that it makes little sense to add to the number of nominal Catholics, or to continue to encourage the notion that baptism—or first Communion, first Confession and Confirmation—are either magical acts that will somehow ensure the child's salvation or what "everyone does" who belongs to a given ethnic subculture—or a combination of both. But how can the quality of a personal commitment be judged, except by such things as regular attendance at Mass and the sacraments—which may or may not be signs of freely chosen, active concern?

Moreover, a great many more or less "nominal" Catholics still feel very strongly about the necessity of baptism for their children's salvation—in however "magical" terms they conceive its effectiveness. It would seem as though the process of transforming many people's notions of what "belonging to the Church" requires in the way of positive commitment to Christian living and Christian parenthood must necessarily be a slow one, requiring much tact and patience in the exercise of authority to achieve what is obviously a laudable purpose. Whether using the desire of parents to have their children baptized as a kind of club to force a profession of faith is the wisest way of introducing people to what will be to them a new notion of the Church and their membership in it, seems to me a very real question.

But, certainly, one can have no such hesitation about *inviting* parents to some form of sacrament-centered education. Many, if not most, are genuinely concerned about their children's receiving the sacraments. They want to understand why traditional rites, customs and rules are being changed and they want to be good parents. Such sacrament-centered education should, of course, be carried on with as much feedback as possible as to whether it is meeting the given persons' real needs, and with their participation in planning and carrying it out. In connection with the particular area of human life which the sacrament is meant to illuminate and celebrate, it could open out to them the dimensions of their basic role in their children's religious education: to help their children mature as human persons who, as Christians, are called to be signs of the grace of Christ at work in the world.

For example, parents expecting their first child might be invited to discuss the impact of this coming event on their relationship to each other, the importance of their attitudes to one another, to life, sexuality, other people, in relation to their child's development. They could be helped to realize the importance of working to create a family community to be a sign and instrument of the Christian community into which this child will be welcomed at baptism, the community which is meant to be a sign of the community of mankind in God's love. Similarly, with parents of children of an age to receive their first Communion or to be introduced to the sacrament of Penance: group discussion with competent resource-persons could help parents better understand their children's psycho-social development and the relationship of their family and personal life and growth to the reality of which the given sacrament is the sign.

One parish recently worked out a program along these lines in preparation for junior high-school students' Confirmation. A group of key couples met with the children's teachers, the priests and the parish staff and decided that:

> for our young people at this stage in their lives, confirmation could not mean making an adult commitment to Christ and Church; it could not mean arriving at Christian maturity. What it could mean, however, would be committing themselves to a new beginning at a new stage in life. What it could mean is the sacramentalizing of a specific "moment"—the adolescent "moment." The adolescent approaches a new threshold in life. Couldn't this peak moment with the identity-fidelity crisis it brings be met with a Christian response? . . . Certainly, then, opportunities must be carefully planned

for adult personal growth (to provide examples of live, visible Christian adulthood) and reawakening to their responsibility for the faith of the young. But what began to take shape was an idea about . . . an experience to be offered to the parents, an opportunity to reaffirm publicly, in the presence of their young, those values and beliefs motivating their own Christian lives.

The parents of the candidates were therefore invited to meetings once a week for six consecutive weeks, with the topics for their discussions paralleling those of the Sunday sermons and of the instruction the young people were receiving. A student-parent panel discussion was also held—at the students' request, based on questions prepared by the young people (e.g., Is Sunday Mass absolutely necessary to good Christian living? If yes, are you saying that a person cannot be a good Christian without living up to his Sunday worship obligation?). Four days before the Confirmation ceremony, "On Sunday morning at the 10.30 Mass, the parents gave their children striking witness to the fact that they were continually trying to live that 'moment' of Confirmation to which their adolescents would respond in just four days" in a "Liturgy of Recommitment by the Adult Faith Community." [5]

True, not a large proportion of the parents of the confirmands attended these meetings, but one might hazard a guess that, in the long run, such a program—freely attended by those who took part in it and enlisting their active cooperation—might have a greater effect, not only on the participants but on the whole parish than would one which parents were forced to attend. Certainly, the idea of making their children's reception of the sacraments an opportunity for Christian growth for the parents as well is an excellent one, and far better than "involving parents" in the old sense. But can growth—or even the opportunity for growth—be forced on people and be effective?

5. See Sister Gloriana Bednarski, "A Total Parish Plan for Confirmation," *The Living Light*, vol. 9, no. 1 (Spring, 1972), in press.

This whole question of authoritarianism on the part of pastors and of religious educators is, of course intimately connected with that of adult religious education of any kind or sort. It seems to be increasingly clear that some form of "participatory democracy," through which people can explore their own needs and decide how best these can be met, is itself a form of education and the key to potential growth and mutual creativity. Some methods of working towards such a mode of operation will be discussed in the next chapter, for in this direction, it seems to me, lies the hope of the future.

"But They Aren't Learning the Basics." "They Aren't Learning Anything."

These are certainly the loudest parental complaints about many of the new religion programs for children and adolescents. One of the bases of both of them is surely the idea that absorbing information about this or that area of human life and thought is the primary objective of education rather than an ancillary one—the idea which most of us were brought up with and which it is so hard to get rid of. In chapter 3, we discussed the crippling effects of this notion, especially today, in any area of education, and it is equally true in religious education. Moreover, what most complainers mean by "the basics" are some abstract formulations of doctrines, the nature and effects of the sacraments, the commandments of God and the Church, etc. But, as was said earlier, experts on children's cognitive development are convinced that forcing them to memorize such formulations before they are capable of handling abstract ideas is not only useless, but may be positively harmful. (This does not of course, apply to poetic and non-verbal communication of the realities which the formulations attempt to express in their own way.)

However, this is by no means to say that there is no place in religious education programs or elsewhere, for information about every aspect of our Catholic Christian heritage, and even for definitions. Centuries ago, the author of *The Imitation of Christ* wrote that it was far better to practice the virtue of humility than to know the definition of it—a dictum with which modern educators would thoroughly agree so far as children are concerned. But, some years ago, Maisie Ward Sheed was discussing the possibility of writing a book on "dangerous half-truths," and included this classic saying as one of them. For, as she said, it is still better both to practice a virtue *and* to know its definition, since this should help one practice it better. However the question is: when would learning the definition be helpful? The answer clearly would seem to be: only when a person is both capable of understanding it and is interested in exploring its implications for his own life.

My husband was once discussing the reorganization of a Catholic college's curriculum with a group of distinguished educators, and remarked that nobody should be able to graduate from a Catholic college who could not give an intelligent answer to the question: "How should your belief in the Trinity influence your behavior on a crowded bus?" After an embarrassed pause, someone asked, "Well, how should it?"

The "new methods" aim to eliminate this dichotomy between "knowing" formulations of doctrine and theological elaborations of them, and daily life and behavior. They try, for example, to give young children a sense of the wonder and presence of God our Source and Goal, God our Way, Truth and Life incarnate in Christ, God our animating Spirit, without using words like "Trinity," "nature," "person," "incarnation," until people are capable of handling such terms effectively—which might be in adolescence or even later. (After all, the New Testament writers managed without them.)

In this aim, these methods follow the directives of the General Catechetical Directory [6] recently issued by the Sacred Congregation of the Clergy and meant to provide guidelines for Episcopal

6. Available from the Office of Publications of the United States Catholic Conference, 1312 Massachusetts Ave., N.W., Washington, D.C. 20005.

Conferences of countries and regions in drawing up their own Directories. One chapter out of four, in one part out of six, is devoted to "The More Outstanding Elements of the Christian Message," whereas two whole parts discuss "Elements of Methodology" and "Catechesis according to Age Levels," and the others various aspects of the context of catechesis—thus making it abundantly clear that "teaching" these outstanding elements may be done by many methods other than that of having children memorize formulations attempting to express them.

But of course, as was said earlier, it is certainly imperative that educators make the effort to help parents understand what they are trying to accomplish in classes using new methods. A lesson for eight-year-olds might include, for example, looking at slides of wind blowing clouds and waves and trees, and then going outdoors to fly paper planes. The purpose of these activities would be to help the children at their own level grow in appreciation of the wonder of wind as a sign of God's Spirit and of our interaction with this infinite vitality of love. But a child cannot and should not be expected to articulate this purpose so, when he comes home and says, "You know, we went out and flew paper planes in religion class today," a parent who had not been previously informed regarding the program could hardly help wondering what on earth this had to do with religious education. (Incidentally, simply to contact parents by the written or spoken word is certainly much better than nothing. But it would be still better if, in a parent-teacher meeting, they could experience the same kind of lesson on their own level and then discuss it.)

One major cause of complaints about children's not learning anything in new religion programs is, then, the parents' unfamiliarity with the aims and methods of the "liberating" kind of education sketched out in chapter 4, as applied to children's religious education. But there are parents who are acquainted with these methods and, whether they approve of them in other areas or not, still want their children taught "the basics" in the way they themselves were taught, primarily by rote memory. One group for instance, as a survey discovered, wanted the local Catholic high schools to use progressive methods in every subject except religion.

Here we come back to the difficulty experienced by so many Catholics, brought up to the idea of an unchanging Church and unchanging formulations of doctrine—the difficulty discussed in chapter 1—of accepting the fact of change along with continuity in the Church, and the relativity of formulations together with the unity of the Christian message. Some people, it seems, can never feel comfortable with this way of looking at Christian faith and life. But perhaps they could nonetheless come to realize that few young people today can find authentic Christianity without it.

In fact, it is the overdose of doctrinal formulations and information about Christian teachings given to so many children in the past, and even today in some places, which makes the question of adequate programs for adolescents even more complicated than it would be otherwise. If the young people have been "turned off" by their previous religion classes and feel that "they have heard all that stuff before," then programs have to take this attitude into account and be as unlike traditional classes as possible—which is what many of the newer programs try to do. On the other hand, perhaps some students are not bored or resentful, and we may hope that their number will increase as time goes on. Some kind of sifting process would therefore seem to be called for in view of planning different programs for different needs.[7]

One solution being used in Catholic schools and CCD programs is to offer a choice among courses, so that the student

7. An initial attempt at such a sifting process, rating students both as to their religious knowledge and their attitudes toward religion, is described in Robert Yorke O'Brien, S.J., "A Solution to Some Problems of a High School Religion Program," *The Living Light*, vol. 8, no. 3 (Fall, 1971), pp. 65 ff.

will feel some freedom and still be given the opportunity to acquire an intellectual understanding of the Christian vocation sufficient for working toward a free adult commitment. Another solution, preferably complementary to such courses, is a once-a-month intensive weekend program, combining various creative activities and disciplined reflection on them with prayer, thus building up the sense of Christian community in a way that an hour's class once a week or three times a week cannot accomplish so well.

No one answer, applicable to all groups and all situations, will ever be found to the question of what programs will best serve the needs of children or adolescents or adults. But Catholic communities will be working toward better solutions as they come to realize more generally and more clearly that learning *about* the Christian religion and the Catholic tradition is only one part, but still a very important part, of a total Catholic religious education, and try to provide this part as and when people are capable of it and would welcome it.

Should We Have Children's Programs at All?

On the other hand, some authorities are proposing, and a considerable number of parents are agreeing with them, that any kind of structured religion programs for children are not only unnecessary but positively harmful, precisely because they equate such programs with teaching abstract formulations of doctrine.[8] When parents with this view come to realize that children cannot handle such formulations and that trying to make them do so may warp their future religious development, they begin to think that their children will do very well, in fact much better, without any structured religious education until

8. It seems to me that Robert O'Neil and Michael Donovan's *Children, Church and God: The Case Against Formal Religious Education* (New York: Corpus Books, 1970) makes this mistake.

adolescence; that the parents—through example, family prayer, and so on—can do all that is needed.

I would entirely agree that it would be far better to have no programs than poor ones. But children might often have quite ambivalent feelings about their parents, and to have religion associated almost exclusively with family life could in some cases have very unfortunate effects. Of course, even the best religion class cannot counterbalance the effect of, for example, a tyrannical or weak father or a too possessive mother on a child's religious development. But it can do something to help him feel that his relationship to God is a reality beyond his feelings about his parents, giving him space to breathe in, so to speak. Moreover, children need to grow in the realization that they belong to a faith-community, a realization which would be fostered by contact with representatives of this community, acting as such, other than their parents.

Another factor to be considered is that children do "theologize" in their own fashion in their middle-childhood years, in the sense of seeking some order in their experience and the meaning of their sense of a Beyond—what is it trying to tell them? In any case, they cannot grow up in a theological vacuum; they inevitably encounter and wonder about other people's explicit or implicit theologizing and its obvious effects—e.g. church buildings, Christmas cribs and carols, biblical references in current songs, etc. They need occasions, then, where it is made easy and natural to ask the questions that occur to them besides those which may be provided in family life.

It seems to me, then, that programs for children based on the approach outlined in chapter 2 can be very helpful to a child's development when these can be well and sensitively carried out. But such programs need not necessarily be planned on the "traditional" basis of once a week throughout the school year through all eight grades. How often for these age-groups a given community can provide *good* programs should be the decisive question.

The Scope of "Religious Education"

It is significant that what used to be called the National Center of the Confraternity of Christian Doctrine (or CCD) recently changed its name to the National Center of Religious Education—CCD. The same change has taken place in many cases with regard to what used to be called diocesan CCD offices, with some of the present Offices of Religious Education having charge of school as well as out-of-school programs. Again, on both the parish and diocesan level a new profession is developing: that of Religious Education Coordinator or Director.

Such changes indicate a widening of the scope of "religious education" far beyond "teaching doctrine" on the part of those who made them. But this very widening causes many problems. For one thing, people in these kinds of jobs who have come to see that the total task of Christian education includes helping one another become more human, in the sense discussed earlier, may find it very difficult to delimit what properly belongs under the heading of "religious education programs."

A person might, for example, decide that some aspect of "humanization" should be made the main purpose of a program conducted under the aegis of "religious education" and, with the authoritarianism we are all liable to now and then, not stop to consult the people concerned, or the parents of children concerned, whether they needed or wanted to be educated in this particular way. For instance, children should certainly be encouraged to draw and paint freely. But if the majority of the children in a given class are already accustomed to this kind of activity at home, both they and their parents will resent it if a major part of their religion classes is spent in drawing or painting whatever they want to. Or again, if the local school or other agency is providing a good drug education program (and there are many poor ones [9]), why start another one under Catholic

9. See *Films on Drugs*, University of California Extension Media Center, 1970. Cited by Janet M. Bennett, *"Fire! Fire!" says Mrs. Maguire.*

auspices? Or if the literature classes in the local high school are cultivating students' abilities to consider the light which outstanding novels and films can shed on the human situation, why try the same thing in an out-of-school religion class?

On the other hand, when essential elements of a human education are not being provided by other agencies in the area, it may well be within the province of the religious educator to do so. For example, the CCD office in Louisville, Kentucky, wrote up a proposal for a program to adapt the methods of "Participatory Training" [10] to poor families. As was said in an earlier chapter, the purpose of this training is "1) to teach people how to learn and how to work together as a learning team; 2) to teach the learning team how to plan a learning activity." Offering an adapted version of this training to "deprived" families would help them begin to consider themselves a "community," and to take shared responsibility in a more conscious and effective way for the tasks and achievements of the family as a whole and of each member. As Nathaniel Greene, the planner of this program, said, "We talk a lot about parents being the primary religious educators of their children; this program is trying to help them." Should not such a program properly be considered "religious education" under these circumstances?

This widening of the scope of "religious education" has thus made it very difficult for professional parish Religion Coordinators or Directors (the terms are practically interchangeable) to define their role in relation to that of the pastor and his priestly assistant(s) and to that of other parish organizations, and to harmonize their role-expectations and those of the people who hired them.[11] Moreover, as this new profession has been developing so rapidly, its members themselves are being forced

---

"Some Reflections on the Current Catechetical Scene," *The Living Light*, vol. 8, no. 3 (Fall, 1971), p. 40.

10. See chap. 4, footnote 17, above.

11. For an attempt to "distinguish in order to unite" these expectations, see Stephen C. Nevin, "Parish Coordinators: Evaluating Tasks and Roles," *The Living Light*, vol. 9, no. 1 (Spring, 1972), in press.

to re-think their role, and also what the most adequate preparation for it should be.

Initially, degrees in religious education were given almost exclusively on the basis of courses in theology, with some additional training in psychology and pedagogy. Now one school of thought, advocated very strongly by James Michael Lee of Notre Dame University,[12] is convinced that religious education belongs primarily in the social-science field, with theology as ancillary. (One major objection to this view, as it seems to me, is that it is a person's theologizing that sets the goals for his teaching and for his use of the social sciences, so that the cultivation of the ability to theologize in the Christian tradition must in some sense be primary in the training of the religious educator.) A third view holds that the emphasis should rather be on a person's maturity as a human being and a Christian, able to live in creative community with others. Many people in the field also consider courses in such techniques as "participatory planning," community organization, and so on, to be as necessary as training in theologizing and in teaching skills.

At the same time, of course, much rethinking is going on about the role of the pastor and of the pastoral ministry in the Church and the kinds of preparation they may call for, and about the role of the "ordinary Catholic" in the ministry of the Church to its own members as well as to society.

All these factors, together with those we have been concerned with throughout this book, indicate the need for each of us to consider our own ministry in relation to those of others—a ministry which, as I hope this book has brought out—must necessarily be educational in some sense, whatever our "state in life" or our occupations. Some lines for such a consideration will be suggested in the next chapter.

12. See his most recent book, *The Shape of Religious Instruction* (Dayton, Ohio: Pflaum, 1971).

8
We're All in This Together

A GREAT JAPANESE PAINTER, Okusai I think it was, remarked at the age of ninety that if he could live for another twenty years he might begin to learn how to paint. This attitude—that learning, change, growth, are possible at any age, is one which, as I hope this book has suggested, we all need to cultivate today and help one another cultivate. It is not an easy attitude to maintain, since it means leaving behind any security that one has "arrived" in any sense, and most of us were brought up to believe that we ought to "arrive" at some kind of material and psychological status and security at least by middle age.

The Second Vatican Council brought out, both in its document on the Church and in its proceedings and their consequences, an idea which many Catholics find as hard to accept as that of continued personal growth: that the Church is a pilgrim Church which must learn and change and grow, leaving behind all securities except the assurance of Christ's presence. And, since the Council also emphasized the fact that we *are* the Church, clergy and laity alike, we are therefore all co-responsible for its continued renewal, for the style and direction of its on-going pilgrimage.

What, then, can we do about our own learning and growth and that of the Church, so as to contribute to the pilgrimage of mankind towards fullness of life?

One fact is becoming increasingly clear both from developments in many sciences and from "the signs of the times": that we need other people in order to learn and grow. This does not mean, of course, that we necessarily have to join a study-group or any other organization. The traditional form of "adult education" now called "self-directed study" in academic circles is still a possibility. But when reading one is involved with other people—with the writer and all those who influenced him. Still more, pursuing any interest fairly consistently usually leads to discovering other people with the same interest, to becoming involved in some kind of community the members of which contribute to one another's growth, and in some kind of action as a result of that growth.

I have found all this to be true in my own life. An initial (and very odd for that time) interest in theology led to a lifetime of "self-directed study" of an increasing number of disciplines (together with finding a husband who shared the same interest and raising a family). At the same time, as part of the same process, it has led me into many kinds of communities of concern, whose members seldom meet together but nonetheless encourage and stimulate one another to continue learning and growing and acting.

Thus belonging to a group that holds some kinds of meetings and engages in some form of common acting is not absolutely essential for mutual creativity. But today, as the substance of traditional communities such as the family, the village, the neighborhood, is as it were leaching away, people seem to feel the need for new forms of visible, tangible communities and for new ways of giving substance to old ones and reality to new ones. As was said in the first chapter, the remarkable spread of many kinds of communes is one example of the first; the rapidly proliferating development of many kinds of techniques to help people get along together, relate to one another on various levels, work together, plan together, organize to change conditions, and so on, illustrates the second.

Christians, of course, have a special need for visible, tangible communities, local incarnations of the community of the Church, whose members are trying to be mutually creative, thus giving witness to what all human communities should aim towards, as well as contributing to their becoming so. We have a special need because we are called to realize explicitly and consciously God's call to all mankind to community with him and with one another, and we have a special obligation to try to form and foster such communities, for our own sake and for that of our witness to the whole human community.

It is significant then, that so many new Christian groups are forming in so many parts of the country. Some of them are "floating parishes," some are "underground churches," some are just groups who meet more or less regularly; some have well-defined aims, some very vague ones; some no other reason for existence than dissatisfaction with any existing "institutional" communities. And there are also the many new experiments with religious community life both within established Orders and outside them—for example, the members of the "Association of Free Monasteries" who have no idea of seeking canonical recognition.

One very interesting six-week experiment, carried out by a temporary community composed of men and women of canonical religious orders under the auspices of the Conference on Religious Development (CORD) in the summer of 1971, might shed light on the requirements of any Christian community which is to be mutually creative, an educating community.

The basic plan was simple: six weeks during which the group would live together, share the daily liturgy and a time of common prayer, with attention focused each week upon a different but progressively related theological theme. Two days each week were spent in seminar sessions concentrated upon the week's theme—a Monday feed-in session and a Thursday feed-back session. . . . We were testing for one element especially: did the participants perceive the content and impact of the seminar sessions as arising from their experience as a here-and-now (though temporary) community, or was the theological study perceived as external. We were testing for the experience of theological study as a learning process integral to the process of being a human community.

Their conclusions were that there are:

three primary emphases through which one can center a personal concern for religious consciousness: *community* as the experiential context of religious values, *theologizing* as the formulation of meanings, and *educating* as communicating through perception.

And all these are in aid of fostering the art of *ministering* which, in turn is an incentive to, and a cause of further learning with these three emphases. But also:

Community at any point on a continuum must be inspired and motivated by integrated persons. These catalysts, these integrated persons, also move along a continuum of experience reaching both outward and inward. No one moves along this path of awareness and commitment unless he, in turn, has been moved by the convictions, by the breadth and depth of the faith experience shared with others.[1]

1. Edward Robley Whitson, "To Move with Others—Beyond Professionalism in Religious Education," *The Living Light*, vol. 9, no. 1 (Spring, 1972), in press.

This may seem like a rather hothouse experiment, carried out under ideal conditions by a selected and dedicated group. But I think that its conclusions are applicable—though in a vast variety of ways—to any kind of Christian community. In fact, many-sided efforts are being made, under various titles and auspices, to foster these elements of Christian community, and herein lies hope for the future.

In discussing these elements and how they may be mutually fostered, I will be using examples of parishes and dioceses. The parish is, of course, the most obvious visible Catholic "community," but very seldom, it seems, in the authentic sense of mutual creativity, of an active sharing of truth and meaning, of educative, mutually developing interaction between persons and groups. Many people, indeed, despair of the geographical parish structure as having any possibilities for creative development. Thus even partially successful efforts to transform parishes into true communities are all the more signs of hope. I trust, then, that the following examples may not only suggest possibilities for parish renewal, and serve as guidelines adaptable to other groups (including families), but may also indicate ways in which other groups might find a ministry within their members' own parishes as well as elsewhere.

The most essential task is that of changing the current model of a parish, so deeply entrenched in many people's minds. (The necessity for such a change applies equally to the family and to educational institutions.) The old ethnic parish was a true community in its own way but, as it ceased to be one, a service-station model took its place. According to this model, now predominant, the pastor, his assistant(s), and other professionals (teachers in the school, religion coordinators), should provide certain services: Mass at convenient times, administration of the sacraments as needed, perhaps various kinds of advice and help, and religious education through a school and/or other programs. The professionals may enlist volunteers—an Altar Society, CCD teachers—but the ordinary parish member thinks of his chief active role as that of paying for the services provided by the professionals.

This model necessarily blocks off the "practice of religion" and "religious education" from the rest of life. It divides the teachers from the learners, the service-providers from the consumers. Thus it makes true community and true religious education impossible, just as segregating teachers and children in schools makes our educational system of such doubtful value. It is because so many parishes have been working with this model that Religion Coordinators or Directors are having such a difficult time. (An informed observer of the current scene estimates that a majority change jobs after one year—some to try again in another parish, many to go into some quite different kind of work.) For many Coordinator/Directors see their task as that of facilitating religious teaching-and-learning in the whole parish, whereas too often the pastor and the people expect them to do all the teaching (and many other tasks) themselves. This model is also what makes "adult education" such a problem: most adults do not want to be "educated" in the sense in which they understand the term, as becoming passive consumers of prepackaged information.

But in the model proposed by the CORD experiment mentioned above, the "catalysts" of the group are themselves involved in its "continuum of experience;" they learn with and from the other members, while they facilitate the on-going learning process of the whole group. In other words, the whole group becomes, and sees itself as an "educating community." Some of its members have the special responsibility of facilitating one or other aspect of its teaching-and-learning, but everyone is involved in both aspects; moreover teaching-and-learning continue through doing, through one or another form of ministry; they are distinguishable but not separable from it.

In a parish, then, which was trying to work along the lines of this educating community model, the pastor would see his role as that of the core, the dynamic center of unity, of the group of catalysts or facilitators who together would form the pastoral team, and of the parish as a whole. This team would then act as catalysts or facilitators for the parishioners' growth in community, for their theologizing and for their continuing education in and through various forms of ministry. And the parishioners would begin to see their role, not as that of taking advantage of opportunities or occasions provided by specialists, but as co-teacher-learner-doers, free to plan, initiate and carry on their own projects, to help one another do so in various kinds of groups, and to call on resource-persons as needed. The members of the pastoral team could act as such resource persons on occasion, but their primary role would be that of facilitating this intra-church ministry through which the members of the community help one another in different ways to "grow up in all things towards Christ," the better to give their witness and service to their society.

On the "service" side of the dominant model, it seems to be mainly Religious Education Directors who have been and are working towards this new model of the educating community. This is probably due to the fact that trying to promote "adult education" almost forces a person to realize that very few adults are interested in any kind of learning unless it meets their felt needs, and that they are more interested the more they are concerned in planning and carrying out what is to be done. Thus an increasing number of parishes and dioceses use questionnaires to ascertain, for example, what areas adults are concerned to learn more about (changes in worship, morality, authority, etc.) and what format they would prefer for learning (lecture, discussion group, in homes or elsewhere). Then the programs offered attempt to respond to these needs and preferences. An example is the program in the Archdiocese of Baltimore called GIFT (Growth In Faith Together), which has three phases: *Research,* consisting in a "Survey of Religious Beliefs and Concerns" sent to every household in the parish; *reflection* in small groups gathered "to identify their questions of faith and to discuss their concerns" which are then presented to the parish priests and voted upon (as to their order of importance) at a General Parish Gathering; and *Response:* two weeks "during which parish priests and invited resource persons conduct educational and liturgical events based on the concerns of the reflection groups. Continuing Response provides educational and liturgical events for months and years to come." [2]

Such a program, obviously, helps those parishioners who participate to begin to realize their own responsibility for identifying their needs in the area of theologizing (and a considerable proportion have done so in the parishes which have used it; in fact the program has been so successful that it is now mandatory for every parish in the Archdiocese to carry it out within the next three years unless excused for some serious reason). At the same time, it builds the parishioners' sense of community, by involving them in a common effort and by the small-group-discussion and General Parish Gathering.

Another and wider kind of effort, attempting to foster all the elements of Christian growth mentioned in the CORD experiment, is "The Year of Adult Response" in the Archdiocese of St. Paul and Minneapolis which was designed "to involve as many adults as possible in focusing on their continuing growth as Christians . . . it is opening avenues leading in all directions." [3] Before the inauguration of the program in the fall of 1971, "preparation sessions were held for volunteers who had committed themselves to one year's work in adult enrichment programs. Planning workshops gave them an adequate measure of security and know-how. They learned how to motivate people, how to recruit other volunteers, how to capitalize on the talent

2. See James M. Schaefer, "GIFT—An Adult Education Program that Works," *The Living Light*, vol. 8, no. 3 (Fall, 1971), p. 77 ff. The survey and other GIFT materials may be obtained from GIFT, 320 Cathedral St., Baltimore, Md. 21201.

3. *Year of the Adult Response—1971–1972* may be obtained from the Department of Adult Education, 251 Summit Ave., St. Paul, Minn. 55102.

in their neighborhoods. They differ from teacher volunteers who work to gain academic knowledge for certification, for they are planners and organizers." [4] These volunteers then act as catalysts and facilitators, helping the people in the parishes to decide on what kind of programs they are interested in and how to carry them out, with a wider range of possibilities from Religious Studies, Spiritual Enrichment, to Drug Education and Social Involvement.

The staff of the Religious Education Office in Davenport is thinking and acting along similar lines:

> They are in the process of growth from a resource organization engaged in broad and direct service programming to a research staff concerned with what processes are involved in freeing local parish communities from the disease of educational passivity. The searching is shifting from a preoccupation with how to do effective teacher training to the development of "models" which stimulate parish activity, confidence and creativity, without our expertise getting in the way.
>
> Since in the diocese, the diocesan staff is seen as resource personnel with answers to problems in religious education, their evolution in this new direction is being deliberately considered and carefully implemented. That is to say, they will continue to service parishes in the resource mode. But their future growth would seem to lie in mutual research and experimentation into whatever is relevant to the vitalization of self-sufficient educational communities. [5]

At the present time, then, a number of Religious Education Directors or Coordinators see their task as that of facilitating, not only the theologizing aspect of a Christian community's life, but the whole process of transforming it into an educating,

4. Loretta Girzaitis, "Developing Professionals: A Personal Search," *The Living Light,* vol. 9, no. 1 (Spring, 1972), in press.

5. See Thomas A. Downs, "The Diocesan Office and Educating Communities," *The Living Light,* vol. 9, no. 1 (Spring, 1972), in press.

mutually creative community. This would certainly seem to be the most essential task to be attempted today in any Christian community, and wherever there are people with the imagination and competence to carry it out, they should be enthusiastically encouraged to do so, under whatever title. After all, as we saw earlier in chapter 2, "religious education" can be understood to mean the whole process of growth of Christian communities.

But it would seem as though the ideal to be worked toward would be a situation in which all the members of a pastoral team or a diocesan staff would, as was said above, understand their role as that of catalysts and facilitators of the Christian community's on-going self-education in one or another area, with the pastor or bishop as its core and center of unity. In fact, skills in community education and organization surely should be part of the education of anyone who is to engage in pastoral work today.

As things are, the initial work of community education or activation might be carried out by the pastor, or the religious educator, or by someone from outside. For example, a number of persons—priests or lay people—might be trained as community educators to go from parish to parish, as the volunteers were trained in the Minneapolis program. Their task would be to help everyone concerned, the pastoral staff and the parishioners, to change from the service-station model to the community-as-educator model, helping people tap their own resources and utilize them. Obviously, the more effectively such a community educator carries out his task, the sooner he works himself out of a job and the community itself takes over. Thus, if he were an expert from outside the parish, he would move on to another. Or if he were the pastor or religious education coordinator, he would resume his on-going role of facilitator and catalyst as part of a pastoral team composed of persons with various competencies.

For example, one member of the team might specialize in helping interested parishioners plan and carry out liturgical celebrations. Another would be responsible for facilitating religious education programs: someone equipped with a solidly based ability to theologize, with teaching skills, and the ability to help others cultivate both. Another member of the team might have a similar role in the parish's service projects, and another be available for pastoral counselling and spiritual direction.

The pastor, then, would see his special role as that of facilitating this whole thrust toward a community of continuing mutual creativity, whatever his competence as a member of the pastoral team. Again, the work of helping people learn to theologize through more or less structured programs such as those suggested in chapter 2 would be seen as an essential aspect of the total work of Christian community education, but not the whole of it. Moreover, the members of the pastoral team would consider themselves as members of the community, learning in and with it. Thus all the interdependent elements mentioned in the CORD experiment described earlier in this chapter would be fostered: community, theologizing, educating as communicating new perceptions gained through learning and action, and ministry or service, both intra-and extra-parochial.

This kind of church organization, whether for a parish or a group of parishes or a diocese, may seem a distant dream. But we can each begin to work towards it by changing the model in our own minds from the service-station to the educating community one and, as far as possible, acting accordingly—whether at present we are on the "servicing" or "consuming" side of the old model. If a group of parents, for example, are unhappy with the religious education provided by their parish, they might draw on their own resources and set up whatever program seemed better to suit their needs.[6]

But it should perhaps be stressed here that becoming a participating member, in this new sense, of a parish or any Christian community need not necessarily mean attending meetings, join-

6. See, for example, Anita Eitler, "A Family Approach to Religious Education," *The Living Light*, vol. 8, no. 4 (Winter, 1971), pp. 81–87.

ing groups and organizations, etc. Congenital non-joiners and persons already overburdened by their work of human service might occasionally be invited to help as resource-persons, for instance, without being made to feel guilty at not being more "involved." Or, again, an ill or elderly person might contribute a great deal to the community simply by personal contacts—and by prayer. A person does not have to add to an already too-complex life in order to help a Christian community's on-going education; he or she may take part in this process on many levels and in many different ways—some more and some less obvious than others.

In any case, the event in which joiners and non-joiners alike can take part is, of course, the celebration of the Eucharist. This is the action in which a Christian community should be most itself, at once demonstrating and cultivating its mutual creativity, theologizing, educating and giving witness. Nearly all the newly formed or forming Christian communities give their dissatisfaction with the Mass as they experience it in their parishes as their main reason for trying some other form of community; however superficial or profound their notions of what a "meaningful" liturgy should be, their instinct that the Eucharist is central to Christian community is surely sound.

For the Eucharist and other sacramental celebrations are the chief means whereby a Christian community realizes its special identity and unity. The more we take part in the work of humanizing our society, the less we experience any kind of ghetto identity as Catholic Christians. We must find a deeper kind, through our shared values and through working together and individually to realize them. But we need a focus for this effort, occasions on which we come together in physical co-presence to celebrate and nourish our faith, hope and love. Sacramental celebrations can become such occasions in fact, as well as theory, if they are prepared for and celebrated so as to focus communities' and individuals' efforts, failures and achievements. Thus the fact that the major themes of Scripture and the liturgy are the major themes of our life-experiences means that the total educational effort of a Christian community can be integrated and leavened by the exploration and celebration of these themes, to help all its members "grow up in all things towards Christ." [7]

The following fairly detailed description of how two priests went about the work of transforming a parish into an educating community is, then, included to illustrate, not only one way of going about this work, but also the essential role of the liturgy in the total process.

The two priests concerned, Fr. David O'Neill and Fr. Thomas Curran, both of New Zealand, had been gaining doctorates at Boston University, in the sociology of religion and in pastoral counseling respectively, and had had many discussions as to the future direction of pastoral work along the lines of community education. When they returned to New Zealand, in January of 1971, they were appointed respectively pastor and co-pastor of a good-sized, mainly lower- and middle-class parish.

> Our studies . . . had left us deeply committed to the community theme as expressed in the documents of the Second Vatican Council. The Council stated quite clearly: "The office of pastor is not confined to the care of the faithful as individuals, but is also properly extended to the formation of a genuine Christian community" (Ministry and Life of Priests, 6).
>
> A second value to which we were committed is that pastoral ministry should center around pastoral care related to the sacraments. The sacraments have a community dimension. They are not merely personal events; they are events in the life of the whole parish community. A program for the devel-

7. The "Coordinated Catechetical Plan" developed by the East Asian Pastoral Institute, described in chapter 2 certainly seems an excellent way of uniting a community in its theologizing in developing current liturgical themes to shed light on current concerns.

opment of a community of faith should use sacramental celebrations as a point of entry into the life of that community.[8]

Their first meeting with the parish council, consisting of
twelve members elected to represent neighborhoods and organizations, "convinced us that there was a genuine desire to re-
vitalize the whole life of the parish." Since Lent was soon to
begin, they proposed that the parish council cooperate with
them in developing a pastoral program for Lent around the
theme of the community's need for penance and new life.

The council decided upon a four-hour workshop on the Monday before Ash Wednesday to help develop a pastoral catechesis of penance. The objectives of the program were:

1. To develop a deeper sense of community awareness
   among parishioners;
2. To search for this awareness in the Christian message, in
   the liturgy of penance, and in a shared devotion to our
   community tasks.
3. To make full use, in a cooperative spirit, of the resources
   available to the parish community.
4. To help build up the community by bringing together
   the priests, religious and group leaders in the parish;
5. To examine together the present needs and hopes of the
   parish community;
6. To discuss practical plans for action to meet these aims.[9]

They then asked the parish council to consider, in small discussion groups of four or five, the qualities they would expect
of an ideal parish, then to look at their own parish and

list what they considered to be the driving forces which were
operating to bring about the ideal they had outlined, and what
were the resisting forces which were hindering it. The princi-

8. Thomas A. Curran, "A Parish Program in Community Education,"
The Living Light, vol. 8, no. 3 (Fall, 1971), pp. 117–118.
   9. *Ibid.*, pp. 118, 119.

pal driving forces were the liturgy, leadership within the parish (particularly from the pastor), education and service to the whole community. The resisting forces were apathy, social stratification, lack of sophistication in the liturgy, lack of leadership within the community, and lack of communication between all the groups in the parish. The next step was to identify, out of the twenty or thirty resisting forces they had brought up, the three or four which were most readily accessible to change.

We were not asking for the *most important* blocks to progress. We were asking for the ones that they considered could be *most* easily changed or removed. After discussing the various possibilities, the council decided that they could do something in the immediate future about revitalizing the parish council itself, about liturgy in the parish, about parochialism and about involving youth in parish affairs.[10]

They then divided into four groups to draw up three action steps which would help in removing or decreasing these blocks to progress, and volunteers were asked to go to work on them—which they did, with gratifying results.

In the meantime, the Lenten program was drawn up and agreed upon, developing such themes as "Taking Away the Sin of the World" (our communal responsibility for the sins of our time; forgiveness in the hope that Jesus gives us); "Sin Can Destroy Love"; "Go, Be Reconciled with Your Brother" (the only way to the Lord of love is the way of mutual forgiveness). These themes were to be developed in preaching, in a variety of liturgical and paraliturgical ways, and in catechetics during the six-week program.

The next step was to involve the two formal religious education agencies, the Catholic schools and the CCD, in this community learning process. A four-day workshop was held for the teachers in the four Catholic schools in the parish—a grade school, an intermediate school, a boys' and a girls' high school.

10. *Ibid.*, p. 119.

As one result, each school took the responsibility for preparing the prayers of the faithful for the Sunday Masses of one week of the Lenten program, following the theme of the week, to be read by students at each Mass, and to prepare and present their own version of the Stations of the Cross on the Thursday night of the week. "The school children had grown up in those years when the Stations were in partial eclipse, and they discovered meaning in them which the adults had long forgotten. They wrote meditations, prayers, songs, and, in one case, even painted their own Stations."

Next the two priests held a workshop with the personnel of the CCD—the executive committee, the teachers and their assistants, the drivers in the car pool and the home visitors. "We wanted CCD to begin to adopt a larger role in making decisions about its concerns and to see itself as part of the whole parish community." This led to two further workshops at the request of the teachers, one inviting the parents to discuss how they would like their children to celebrate their first confession, and a similar one on first Communion.

Another workshop was held with the Young Christian Workers who had been discouraged at the nonsuccess of their efforts to kindle some enthusiasm in the parish. They had been tending to separate themselves from the parish and have meaningful liturgies and meetings for themselves. The idea that they formed a vital element in the parish and should exercise it began to break down their isolation. As a result:

> They approached the Catholic Women's League and arranged a meeting between the two groups to discuss the "generation gap." They became involved with the League and other groups in the parish in arranging a parish social and dance, which was regarded as the best in years, for the benefit of some needy families in the parish. Because we had no housekeeper in the rectory, they volunteered to provide a phone-answering service each evening during the week. This has

made for very vital contact between them and the priests of the parish. As part of the Lenten program, they prepared a Stations of the Cross which very dramatically reflected their concern with the uncaring attitude of their elders. They now want another workshop to assess their progress and to plan for future involvement.[11]

Next the two priests approached the already "caring" members of the parish: the St. Vincent de Paul Society, the Legion of Mary, the Catholic Women's League, and the Sisters from the local Catholic hospital. They discussed how the parish was caring for the sick and the shut-ins and how it could get done better. The results were the formalizing of a liaison between all the groups in the city concerned with the care of the sick, and requests for training courses in how to give more effective help.

The parish council then asked for a workshop on liturgy for the parishioners, which discussed how to make liturgical events come alive through preparation and celebration. The priests have also become involved with the high school students in preparing liturgies with them for special events. And, since other parishes have heard of this program of pastoral renewal, Frs. Curran and O'Neill have been overwhelmed with requests to run similar programs elsewhere and to conduct workshops for priests on this pastoral approach.

> In our own parish, the religious educators have entered into the whole program enthusiastically. They, too, feel that something has happened here in the last few months. They feel that they are not out on a limb anymore—they are part of the whole community of faith. They feel that the community is beginning to take an interest in what they are doing in a way they have never done before.[12]

11. *Ibid.*, p. 124.
12. *Ibid.*, p. 130.

Much of what we have been doing is already being carried out in some emergent ways in Christian communities; often all that is needed is to coordinate a variety of community activities which have not been seen in terms of their educational potential. Through this coordination, they can be built into a conscious community drive which enriches them with the deep elements of the community's message and hope.

To many pastors and religious educators this approach of ours comes as a delightful surprise for which they have been waiting. So many people have been telling them that the day of the parish and of catechetics is over; we say to them that we are only beginning to realize the potential of our existing structures of Christian community. We say to them that once these existing structures come alive to their own delightful existence, their possibilities for growth in the Spirit and for the development of new forms of life are beyond our present imagining.[13]

To the discouraged American pastor, religious educator, or "ordinary" Catholic, these two priests may seem far too optimistic about the potentialities of such a "community education" approach. It is quite true that New Zealand is not afflicted with our tremendous problems (although "apathy" seems to be a complaint common to both countries). It is also true that these two priests are both talented persons who had equipped themselves with the skills required for community development. Nonetheless, community development is one of the fastest-growing disciplines and arts of our times, these same skills can be acquired by others.

Another objection, to some readers, might be that these two priests were mainly concerned with very "churchy" business, and pretty old-hat church business at that. But the precise point is that they were trying to infuse the existing practices and organizations with a new spirit: not "This is the way we

13. David P. O'Neill, "The Community as Educator: A New Model for Catechetics," *The Living Light*, vol. 8, no. 3 (Fall, 1971), pp. 21–22.